# *North a₁*

## ELIZABETH GASKELL

Level 6

Retold by Mary Tomalin
Series Editors: Andy Hopkins and Jocelyn Potter

**Pearson Education Limited**
Edinburgh Gate, Harlow,
Essex CM20 2JE, England
and Associated Companies throughout the world.

ISBN: 978-1-4058-6781-8

This edition first published by Pearson Education Ltd 2008

1 3 5 7 9 10 8 6 4 2

Text copyright © Pearson Education Ltd 2008

Set in 11/14pt Bembo
Printed in China
SWTC/01

The authors have asserted their moral rights in accordance
with the Copyright Designs and Patents Act 1988

Produced for the Publishers by
Ken Vail Graphic Design

Published by Pearson Education Limited in association with
Penguin Books Ltd, and both companies being subsidiaries of Pearson PLC

**Acknowledgements**
The publisher would like to thank the following for their kind permission
to reproduce their photograph:
BBC Photo Library: pg x
Every effort has been made to trace the copyright holders and we apologise in
advance for any unintentional omissions. We would be pleased to insert the
appropriate acknowledgement in any subsequent edition of this publication.

For a complete list of the titles available in the Penguin Readers series please write to your local
Pearson Longman office or to: Penguin Readers Marketing Department, Pearson Education,
Edinburgh Gate, Harlow, Essex CM20 2JE

# *Contents*

# Introduction

*Mr Thornton ran back up the steps to Margaret.*

*'I'm all right,' she said, and fainted.*

*He picked her up and carried her, still unconscious, into the dining-room. There, he laid her on the sofa and cried passionately, 'Oh, Margaret! No one knows what you mean to me! You are the only woman I have ever loved!'*

*North and South* takes place against the background of the industrial north, in mid-nineteenth-century England. It tells the story of Margaret Hale, a beautiful, intelligent, proud young woman from an upper-class family, admired and loved by everyone who knows her. Margaret's father is a clergyman in the south of the country, but when the family's circumstances change, they move from their beautiful, isolated village to Milton-Northern, a dirty, smoky city in the north, where cotton manufacturing is the main industry.

There, Margaret meets a wealthy mill owner, Mr Thornton. Margaret, who has been brought up to despise people who make money from commerce, dislikes him immediately, and finds him hard and unsympathetic towards his workers. But the mill owner, while seeing Margaret as unpleasantly proud, cannot stop himself from falling in love with her. The novel follows the ups and downs of their relationship as Margaret undergoes a series of personal tragedies and the mill workers strike, with dramatic consequences for Mr Thornton. The changes in outward circumstances are mirrored by great changes in both Margaret and Mr Thornton. Another man, a clever lawyer called Henry Lennox, is also in love with Margaret. Is it possible for either man to win her?

*North and South* was published in serial form between 1854 and 1855, and in book form in 1855. The relationship between Margaret Hale and Mr Thornton, which lies at the heart of the novel, symbolises a very important issue – the difference between the north of England, where industry is changing the cities and countryside, and the south, which remains mostly agricultural and where the upper classes live lazy, unproductive lives. Margaret and her family are representatives of the southern upper classes; they find the move to the industrial north very difficult, and there are tragic consequences for both gentle Mr Hale and the over-sensitive Mrs Hale. For much of her childhood, Margaret lived in London with her aunt's family, and her aunt and Margaret's pretty cousin, Edith, are amusing but charming examples of the lazy rich.

Other important characters include Mrs Thornton, the mill owner's severe mother, who dislikes Margaret immediately, and Margaret's only real friends in Milton-Northern – a mill worker, Nicholas Higgins, and his sick daughter, Bessy. Finally, Margaret's brother, Frederick, and Mr Hale's old friend, Mr Bell, also have small but significant parts to play in the story.

Elizabeth Cleghorn Stevenson was born in 1810 in London. Her mother, who came from a well-connected middle-class family, died when Elizabeth was a baby, and her father, a clergyman and writer called William Stevenson, remarried. Elizabeth spent much of her childhood in a town called Knutsford, where she was brought up by her aunt and lived very happily, surrounded by caring relatives. Elizabeth's family were Unitarians, a form of Christianity that was unusually tolerant for that period and that emphasised the importance of improving social conditions for the poor. It was very influential in forming Elizabeth's character and attitudes.

In 1832 Elizabeth married William Gaskell, a Unitarian

clergyman, writer and lecturer. The couple settled in Manchester and had four children there. Besides doing work among the sick and the poor, the Gaskells lived a very social life, and their friends included great writers and people who, like the Gaskells, were working among the poor.

Gaskell started writing short stories quite early in her writing career but it was the death of her little son that caused her to write her first novel, *Mary Barton* (1848), at the age of thirty-eight, as a way of taking her mind off her grief. The novel was a success and was admired by the important writer Charles Dickens, and between 1851 and 1853 Gaskell's second novel, *Cranford*, was published at irregular intervals in Dickens's magazine, *Household Words*.

Gaskell's next novel, *Ruth*, was published in 1853, and was followed by *North and South*. *The Life of Charlotte Brontë* came out two years later, in 1857. Gaskell's last novel, *Wives and Daughters*, was published in 1866, after her death in 1865.

Elizabeth Gaskell was a lively, amusing, very charming woman, with a huge enjoyment of life and people. She had many friends in London, Europe and the United States and was very involved in the political, religious and scientific issues of the time. She died of a heart attack on 12 November 1865.

Until quite recently, Elizabeth Gaskell was known as 'Mrs Gaskell', a name that reflected her reputation as a writer of gentle, uneventful, easy-to-read novels. This was largely due to the success of *Cranford*, her most popular book during her lifetime. Based on Knutsford, the town where Gaskell was brought up, *Cranford* is a delightful, gently amusing picture of small-town life. But Gaskell wrote fiction of great variety and *Mary Barton*, her first novel, could not have been more different. Due to the influence of Unitarianism, the author was very committed to improving conditions for the poor, and like

*North and South*, the story takes place in a northern city among working-class people. The book was violently attacked by newspapers but was also much admired.

*Ruth* was another novel about the working class, centring on a 15-year-old orphan who has a child outside marriage. Gaskell's courageous aim was to show how easy it was for young girls to be used by wealthy men, but the book shocked many readers.

In 1850 Mrs Gaskell became a good friend of Charlotte Brontë, one of the nineteenth century's greatest writers. Gaskell's *The Life of Charlotte Bronte*, written after Brontë's death, was received with great interest. The book played an important part in building Brontë's reputation and is regarded today as an excellent source of information about her.

*Wives and Daughters*, Gaskell's last novel, concerns two middle-class families in a country town, and shows Gaskell at her best as a natural storyteller and wonderfully sharp observer of country life and characters.

In *North and South*, the conditions of the cotton industry workers and their relationship with their employers are important subjects of the book. Milton-Northern, where the story takes place, is in fact the city of Manchester. Manchester was at the centre of the Industrial Revolution, which began in the last quarter of the eighteenth century and continued through the nineteenth century, transforming Britain into a country where goods were mass produced in factories using mechanical means. The most important industries were the cotton and wool industries, and these were based in northern towns whose populations increased rapidly as a result. Conditions among the factory workers were bad. In *North and South*, Gaskell uses the Higgins family to show the problems of the factory workers, their low wages, and their fight to talk with the cotton mill owners as equals.

In the novel Mr Hale, Margaret's father, is a clergyman who develops such doubts about the Church of England that he feels forced to leave it, move to Milton-Northern and find work there as a tutor. In introducing this issue to the story, Gaskell was strongly influenced by Unitarianism which, although Christian, was in many ways different from the Church of England.

Also important to Unitarianism was its emphasis on the importance of upbringing. In *North and South* Margaret is a very kind and loving person and has been brought up to visit the poor and sick, but her upbringing has also taught her to despise commerce, which to some extent explains her dislike of Mr Thornton. Part of Margaret's journey in the novel is to learn to respect people who are involved in trade, and to become less proud. Similarly, Mr Thornton has been brought up by his mother to despise people who are not successful, and this explains his contemptuous attitude towards his workers. Slowly, Mr Thornton begins to realise that the workers have human feelings as he does. He and Nicholas Higgins become friendly and he becomes persuaded of the importance of employers and workers 'talking freely to each other'.

These changes in Margaret and Mr Thornton reflect the changes that Gaskell wanted to see in society: the northern mill owners treating the workers better, and the south learning to respect the part that industry played in making the country rich. In *North and South*, the author brilliantly combines the love story between two very strong, seemingly very different people and the social issues that were important to her.

# Chapter 1   A Wedding

'Edith,' said Margaret gently, 'Edith!'

But her cousin had fallen asleep. She lay curled up on the sofa in one of the sitting-rooms of the house in Harley Street, looking very lovely in her white dress. The two girls had grown up together, but Edith was getting married in a few days, and it was only now, when she was going to lose her, that Margaret realised how beautiful and sweet her cousin was. They had been talking about Edith's future life on the Greek island of Corfu, where she would live with Captain Lennox after the wedding. But now she had fallen asleep, and Margaret, who had wanted to discuss her own future, had no one to talk to.

Despite the lack of a listener, Margaret's thoughts were happy ones. For the last ten years, her Aunt Shaw's house in London had been her home. But soon she was going to return to the country vicarage where her parents lived, and where she had spent her holidays. She was looking forward to the change, although she regretted the separation from her aunt and cousin.

She was thinking dreamily of the vicarage when Mrs Shaw called out from the room next door. She had invited some neighbours to dinner, and the ladies were talking in the sitting-room while their husbands remained in the dining-room.

'Edith! Edith!'

Margaret rose and went next door.

'Edith is asleep, Aunt Shaw. Can I help?'

All the ladies said, 'Poor child!' on receiving this news, and the little dog in Mrs Shaw's arms began to bark excitedly.

'Be quiet, Tiny, you naughty little girl! I wanted to ask Edith to bring down her Indian shawls. Would you mind fetching them, Margaret?'

Margaret went up to the room at the top of the house where

the shawls were kept. Nine years ago, when she had first arrived in Harley Street, this room had been her bedroom. She remembered her first meal up there, away from her father and aunt, who were eating below. Margaret had always had her meals with her father and mother. The eighteen-year-old girl remembered how she had cried that first night, hiding her face under the bedclothes. Now she had learnt to love her bedroom, and she looked round regretfully, knowing that she was leaving it forever.

She carried the shawls downstairs, and as Edith was still asleep, her aunt asked her to put them on. The long, heavy shawls looked better on Margaret, who was tall and stately, than they would have looked on Edith, who was much shorter. Mrs Shaw was adjusting a shawl around Margaret's shoulders when the door opened and Captain Lennox's brother, Mr Henry Lennox, came in. Margaret looked at Mr Lennox with a laughing face, certain that he would be amused by her situation.

Almost immediately, Edith appeared, shaking her pretty curls. She had a hundred questions to ask Henry, but he soon came and sat next to Margaret, as she had known he would. Margaret's face lit up with an honest, open smile. Henry Lennox liked and disliked almost the same things that she did, and now she was certain to have a pleasant evening.

'Well, I suppose you are all very busy indeed – with ladies' business, I mean. Very different to my business, the law.'

'Indian shawls are very lovely.'

'And their prices are good, too. But is this not your last dinner party before the wedding on Thursday? You have been very busy recently.'

'Yes,' replied Margaret. 'I wonder if it is possible to have a quiet time before a wedding.'

'What would *your* wedding be like?'

'Oh, I have never thought much about it. I would like it to be a fine summer morning; and to walk to church through shady trees. It is natural for me to think of Helstone church, rather than a London one.'

'Tell me about Helstone. Is it a village or a town?'

'Oh, I don't think you could call it a village. There is a church, with a few houses near it – cottages, really – with roses growing all over them.'

'It sounds like a village in a children's story.'

'It is,' replied Margaret eagerly. 'It's like a village in a poem.'

'It sounds lovely. What is the vicarage like?'

'Oh, please don't ask me to describe my home. It's much too difficult.'

'Margaret, don't be cross with me!'

'I'm not cross with you,' said Margaret, looking directly at him with her large, soft eyes.

'Then tell me what you do there. How do you fill your day?'

'I walk a lot. We have no horse, not even for Father.'

'Do you go to dances?'

'Oh, no, nothing like that. We don't have the money.'

'I can see you won't tell me anything. Before the holiday ends, I think I will visit you, and see what you really do there.'

'I hope you will. Then you will see how beautiful Helstone is.'

Tall, handsome Captain Lennox, who had just arrived, came over to greet his brother, with Edith smiling proudly by his side. The two men shook hands and Mrs Shaw welcomed the Captain in her gentle way. Her husband had died many years ago, but she lived a very comfortable life. Lately, she had been worrying about her health, and she started a conversation with the Captain about the possibility of spending the winter in Italy, where it was warmer.

Mr Henry Lennox leaned against the wall, amused by the family scene. Unlike his brother, he was not handsome, but he had a clever, interesting face and people liked him. He was enjoying watching the two cousins as they arranged the table for tea. Edith was doing her best to show the Captain what a good wife she would be, but he noticed that Margaret was much more efficient.

## Chapter 2  Helstone

It was the second half of July when Margaret returned home. The trees were a dark, shadowy green; the plants below caught the sunlight as it came through the leaves, and the weather was hot and still. Margaret took long walks with her father, taking pleasure in the sweet forest smells and the wild, free-living creatures that she saw there. This life – at least, these walks – were just as Margaret had hoped. She loved her forest and had good friends there; she nursed their babies, read to the old people and brought food to the sick. Her outdoor life was perfect. Her indoor life had its disadvantages.

On arriving home she had immediately realised that all was not as it should be. Her mother, always so kind and loving towards her, from time to time seemed deeply discontented. Mrs Hale said that the forest, so near to the house, affected her health, but her biggest complaints were the family's lack of money and her husband's low position in the Church of England. When she mentioned the subject, Mr Hale would reply sadly that as long as he could do his duty in little Helstone, he was thankful, but there were lines of anxiety on his face that had not been there before, and each day he seemed more lost and confused.

Margaret was unprepared for these long hours of discontent. She had known that she would have to give up many luxuries when she returned to Helstone, and she had quite enjoyed the idea. There had been a few complaints from her mother when

Margaret had spent her holidays at home before, but because the memory of those times was generally happy, she had forgotten the small, less pleasant details.

Autumn rains came in the second half of September and Margaret often had to stay in the house. Helstone was at some distance from any neighbours of a similar social position.

'It is undoubtedly one of the most isolated places in England,' said Mrs Hale sadly. 'If only we were within walking distance of the Stansfields and the Gormans.'

'The Gormans?' said Margaret. 'Are those the Gormans who made their fortune in trade in Southampton? I'm glad we don't visit them. I don't like people in trade. I think it's much better for us to know poor country people, people who do not claim to be better than they are.'

'You must not be so hard to please, Margaret, dear,' said Mrs Hale, secretly thinking of a young and handsome Mr Gorman whom she had once met.

'That's not true! I like all those who work on the land. I'm sure you don't want me to admire butchers and bakers – people like that, do you?'

'But the Gormans were neither butchers nor bakers, but very respectable carriage-builders.'

'Nevertheless, carriage-building is a trade, and rather a useless one, in my opinion. I would much prefer to walk than travel in a carriage.'

And Margaret did walk, in spite of the weather; she was so happy outdoors, at her father's side, that she almost danced. But the evenings were rather difficult to fill pleasantly. Immediately after tea her father disappeared into his small library, and she and her mother were left alone. Her mother had never enjoyed books much, and when Mrs Hale began to compare her sister's comfortable life in London with her own life at the vicarage, Margaret would stop talking and listen to the rain as it fell on the sitting-room window. Once or twice she wondered if she could ask about a subject of great importance to her – her older brother Frederick. He had joined the navy some years ago, and had taken part in a mutiny, with the result that he was now unable to return to England, as he would be arrested if he did. Margaret very much wanted to ask where Frederick was now and what he was doing, but an awareness that her mother's bad health dated from the time of the mutiny made her unwilling to do so. Similarly, her father's anxious face made her pause and turn away from the subject each time she approached it.

Frederick's room was kept exactly as he had left it and was regularly cleaned by Dixon, Mrs Hale's servant. Dixon lovingly remembered the day when she had first been employed to look after pretty Miss Beresford, as Mrs Hale had been called then. Dixon had never thought that Mr Hale was good enough for her dear lady and considered that he had caused her much heartache; she saw herself as Mrs Hale's only protector. Frederick had always been her favourite and her rather stiff manner softened a little when she went in each week to tidy his room.

Margaret felt sure that there had been some news of Frederick, unknown to her mother, which was making her kind and gentle father anxious. Often, in conversation, his mind seemed elsewhere, and he spent more time than usual in his study. But when fine weather came in the second half of October, her worries disappeared and she thought of nothing except the beauty of the forest. She was preparing to take her artist's notebook and go drawing in the forest when Dixon threw the sitting-room door open and announced, 'Mr Henry Lennox.'

The sun shone through the window onto Margaret's face as she walked forwards to shake hands with him.

'I am so glad you have come,' she said.

'Did I not say that I would?' he asked. 'I have a little note from Edith. Ah, here it is.'

'Oh! Thank you!' exclaimed Margaret, and went to tell her mother that Mr Lennox had arrived.

When she had gone, Mr Lennox began to look around in his sharp-eyed way. The little sitting-room was looking its best in the morning sunlight; the window was open and roses crept around the corner, while the garden was bright with flowers of every colour. But the brightness outside made the colours inside seem faded. The carpet was old and the house was smaller than he had expected, as Margaret herself seemed so queenly.

'It's as she said, they have very little money,' he thought.

Margaret returned with her mother, who greeted Mr Lennox with great friendliness, and it was agreed that the couple should go to draw in the forest and then return for lunch. Margaret led Mr Lennox through the forest to two little cottages; there, they took out their notebooks and began to draw the pretty scene. When the time came to show each other what they had done, Margaret discovered that Mr Lennox had drawn her.

'I hardly dare tell you how much I like this picture,' he said.

Margaret turned away to pack up her notebook and pencils, and Mr Lennox was not quite sure whether she had heard his words. They returned to the vicarage, and the conversation at lunch flowed quietly and pleasantly. After the meal, he suggested that they should walk in the garden.

'What a perfect life you seem to live here,' he said, looking up at the tall forest trees that enclosed the garden like a nest.

'Please remember that our skies are not always blue. We have rain and even storms sometimes! Although I do think that Helstone is about as perfect as any place in the world.'

'I almost wish, Margaret,' said Mr Lennox, and then hesitated.

It was so unusual for the clever lawyer to hesitate that Margaret looked up at him questioningly.

'Margaret,' Mr Lennox continued, taking her hand, 'I wish you didn't like Helstone so much and that you missed your friends in London more – enough to make you listen more kindly to someone who is not wealthy, it is true, but who does love you, Margaret.'

Margaret made a strong effort to be calm, and then said, 'I did not know that you cared for me in that way. I have always thought of you as a friend.'

'But may I hope that at some time you will think of me as a lover?'

Margaret was silent for a minute or two, trying to discover the truth in her own heart before she replied. Then she said, 'I have only ever thought of you as a friend – I am sure I could never think of you as anything else. Let us both forget that this conversation has taken place.'

Mr Lennox paused before he replied. Then in a colder voice, he said, 'Of course, as this conversation is rather unpleasant to you, I will try to forget it.'

'You are upset,' Margaret said sadly, 'but how can I help it?'

She looked so sad as she said this that he struggled for a moment with his real disappointment, and then said more cheerfully, but still with a little hardness in his voice, 'I am not known to be a romantic man – and the only time that I allow myself to be so, I am rejected. It was madness to think that I – a poor lawyer – could hope to marry.'

The whole tone of these words annoyed Margaret and reminded her of why she could not accept him, and it was fortunate that Mr Hale appeared just then, and a lighter conversation began. Margaret said little, wondering when Mr Lennox would go. He too was anxious to leave, but to save his self-respect began talking in a bored kind of way about his life in London. Mr Hale was puzzled; this was not the man he had met in the city and at lunch that day. It was a relief to all of them when Mr Lennox said that he needed to leave immediately in order to catch the five o'clock train.

At the last moment, Henry Lennox's real self broke through.

'Margaret, don't dislike me – I have a heart, though I pretend that I do not. I believe I love you more than ever – if I do not hate you – for the disdain on your face as you have listened to me during this last half hour. Goodbye, Margaret – Margaret!'

♦

He was gone. The house was locked up for the evening. Margaret sat alone by the fire in the sitting-room, with unlit candles on the table behind her, thinking about the day, the happy walk, the drawing in the forest, the cheerful lunch, and the uncomfortable, miserable walk in the garden. She felt very unhappy that she had had to refuse him, but what else could she have done when, moments after her refusal, he had spoken as if success in life was the only thing that mattered to him? Oh dear! She could have loved him so much if only he had been different. Then she thought that, after all, perhaps he had talked in that cold, hard way to hide his disappointment. She was still considering this when Mr Hale entered, sighing deeply.

'Margaret,' he said at last, in a sudden, desperate way, 'can you come into my study? I want to speak to you about something very serious.'

In the study, Mr Hale made Margaret take a chair next to him. He stirred the fire and then said shakily, 'Margaret! I am going to leave Helstone.'

'Leave Helstone, Father! But why?'

'Because I can no longer be a clergyman in the Church of England.'

Margaret's immediate response was a feeling of shock and disbelief. 'Why? Why can you no longer be a clergyman? Is it because of Frederick?'

'It is not about Frederick. It is all me. For a long time now I have had serious doubts about the authority of the Church.

These doubts have torn me in two and are so great that I feel I have no choice. I must leave.'

'But Father, have you truly considered the consequences?' asked Margaret, bursting into tears.

Mr Hale rose and walked up and down the room, talking to himself in a low voice. Finally, he said, 'Margaret, I have thought about it for a long time. I must do what my heart and mind tell me. I have arranged things so that we will be leaving Helston in a fortnight.'

Margaret sat as still as stone. 'In a fortnight! Where will we go?'

'To Milton-Northern,' her father answered lifelessly.

'Milton-Northern! The manufacturing town in Darkshire?'

'Yes,' he answered in the same depressed way. 'You remember Mr Bell, an old friend of mine at Oxford University – he teaches at the university now. I wrote to him about my troubles. His home town is Milton-Northern and he owns property there which has greatly increased in value since Milton has become such a large manufacturing town. He feels certain that I can earn a living there as a private tutor.'

'A private tutor!' cried Margaret scornfully. 'Are manufacturers interested in studying Ancient Greek literature?'

'Oh,' said Mr Hale, 'some of them really seem to be fine fellows. Mr Bell has recommended me to a Mr Thornton, a tenant of his, and a very intelligent man, apparently.'

'And Mother knows nothing about this?' asked Margaret fearfully.

'Nothing. Poor, poor Maria! Margaret – I dare not tell her!'

'No,' said Margaret sadly, 'I will do it. Oh, Father,' she cried, 'tell me it is all a terrible dream! You do not really mean it!'

Mr Hale sat perfectly still as she spoke. Then he looked her in the face, and said slowly, 'You must not deceive yourself, Margaret. I do mean it.'

He looked at her for some moments and she gazed back. Then she rose and, without a look or a word, left the room.

That night, Margaret sat by her bedroom window, looking out at the brightly lit church, too full of sorrow to cry, but with a cold pain in her heart that made her feel old and hopeless; the afternoon spent with Mr Lennox seemed like a dream. The hard reality was that because her father had doubts about the authority of the Church, their whole life was going to change. Margaret felt as she never had before, completely alone. That night she dreamt that Henry Lennox fell from a high tree and was killed. In the morning she woke feeling exhausted, and the awful reality came back to her.

At breakfast, the fine autumn morning made Mrs Hale feel particularly well and she talked happily, planning visits to the villagers. Mr Hale left, saying he would be out for the whole day. Unlike her father, who would have postponed telling the bad news as long as possible, Margaret took a deep breath and asked her mother to walk with her in the garden. There, Margaret told her about Mr Hale's decisions and his plan to leave Helstone.

At first her mother did not believe her. 'He would surely have told me before this!' she cried.

But when Margaret insisted that they were going to leave Helstone in a fortnight, her mother started to cry quietly, unable to bear the thought of living in a manufacturing town.

'But think of the shame!' she whispered. 'Your father is going to leave the Church! No one we know will want to know us!'

For the rest of that day, Margaret never left her mother. When evening came and Mr Hale returned, his face grey and fearful, his wife threw herself on him and burst into tears, crying, 'Oh, Richard, Richard, you should have told us sooner!'

On hearing this, Margaret left the room and ran up to her bedroom, where she cried bitterly for many hours. But heartbroken as she was, it immediately became clear that her parents were depending on her to make the necessary arrangements for the move to Milton-Northern. Mr Hale was so depressed that he was unable to make any decisions, while Mrs Hale now became really ill and had to spend most of each day in bed. A fortnight was a very short time, and Margaret felt that a great weight had suddenly been thrown upon her shoulders. However, with Dixon's help she began to plan the move.

## Chapter 3  The Move to Milton-Northern

The Hale family left Helstone early one morning to take a train to London. The vicarage, half-covered with roses, looked lovelier than ever in the morning sun and they found it hard to believe they would never see it again. Margaret, who was looking very pale, appeared calm, but her heart was aching. She leaned back in her seat and shut her eyes, and the tears rolled slowly down her cheeks.

They spent a night in London at a quiet hotel and the next day took the train to Heston, a small seaside town about twenty miles from Milton-Northern. Margaret's plan was that her mother and Dixon could stay there while she and her father went to Milton-Northern to look for a house. They found clean, cheerful rooms in Heston, and she felt able to rest at last.

But the future must be met, however difficult it may be. One morning, Margaret and her father set off for Milton-Northern. As they approached the town they saw that a dark grey cloud hung over it, and the air started to taste and smell slightly of smoke. Soon they were travelling through long, straight streets of small brick houses. Huge factories sent out clouds of black smoke, and the streets were crowded with people.

They found their hotel, which was near the centre of the

town, and left immediately to begin their search. There was not much money to spend on rent, and it was difficult to find a house that was big enough for their needs.

After some hours, Margaret said, 'I think we should go back to the second house, the one in Crampton – that was the name of the suburb, I think.'

'But the colours! And the wallpaper!'

'Surely you can ask the landlord to repaper one or two of the rooms? And the bookshelves will hide some of the walls.'

'Then you think we should take it? If you do, I will take you back to the hotel and you can have lunch and rest while I visit the landlord. I only hope he will agree to repaper the rooms.'

As Margaret entered the hotel, a waiter came to tell her that Mr Thornton was waiting in their rooms to see them. Margaret went in to meet him in her usual fearless way; she was used to London society and was not at all shy. Mr Thornton was much more surprised and uncomfortable than she was. Instead of a quiet, middle-aged clergyman, here was a young woman who was very different to those he usually met. She wore a simple, dark silk dress and a large Indian shawl that made her look like an eastern queen. Her gaze was direct and completely uninterested.

'Mr Thornton, I believe,' said Margaret. 'Will you sit down? My father will return soon. He has gone to see Mr Donkins, the landlord of a house in Crampton that my father wishes to take.'

Mr Thornton had promised Mr Bell that he would do his best to help Mr Hale, and he had been to look at the house in Crampton. He had thought that it was perfect, but now that he had met Margaret, he was not so sure. Margaret's short upper lip, strong chin and the way she moved her head and body always made strangers think that she was haughty. She sat directly opposite Mr Thornton, and he had to admit that she was very beautiful, with her white neck and graceful curves.

But her obvious lack of interest made him feel like a rough, uncivilised fellow, and he was not sure he liked her. He thought that her quiet, calm manner was rather disdainful, and he was telling himself that he would leave, when Mr Hale entered and apologised in his pleasant way for not being there to meet him.

The two men began to talk about their friend, Mr Bell, and Margaret moved to the window and watched the street.

'Margaret,' said Mr Hale suddenly, 'the landlord refused to change the wallpaper.'

'Oh dear!' she said and began to think of ways of hiding it.

Her father invited Mr Thornton to have lunch with them, but since Margaret did not add her own invitation, Mr Thornton felt unable to accept. He left, feeling more uncomfortable than ever in his life before.

When they returned to Heston, Mrs Hale was full of questions about how they had spent the day.

'And what is Mr Thornton like?' she asked.

'Oh, I don't know,' said Margaret, who was feeling tired. 'He is a tall, broad-shouldered man of about thirty, I think, with a face that is not ugly but not handsome either. He is not quite a gentleman – but one would not expect that.'

'He is not a coarse man,' said her father.

'Oh no!' said Margaret. 'His expression is much too powerful and determined. He looks like what he is – a great tradesman.'

'Don't call the Milton cotton manufacturers tradesmen, Margaret,' said her father. 'They are very different.'

'Are they? I use the word for those who have something to sell. Oh, Mother! You must prepare yourself for the sitting-room wallpaper! Pink and blue roses, with yellow leaves!'

But when they moved to the house in Milton, the landlord had changed the wallpaper. They did not know that when Mr Thornton, the wealthy manufacturer, asked for something to be done, people hurried to obey.

It was difficult for the family to feel comfortable in their new home. The thick yellow November fogs crept up to the windows and through every open door. Mrs Hale was miserable and caught a bad cold. Mr Hale was equally miserable and came to Margaret for sympathy, but she was unable to comfort him. The move to Milton had spent nearly all their money. Here they were and here they must remain. At night, when Margaret realised this, she felt quite despairing. The heavy, smoky air hung in her bedroom, and all she could see from her window was a blank wall. A letter from Edith arrived describing her new life in her pretty house overlooking the sea; it was a life without any problems. Margaret wondered if her old friends thought about her at all. What would her life have been like if she had agreed to marry Henry Lennox? But she knew he would have found it very difficult to accept her father's changed position in society.

Mr Hale found several pupils, recommended by either Mr Bell or Mr Thornton. They were mostly schoolboys, and Mr Thornton was probably the oldest of Mr Hale's students. He was certainly the favourite. Mr Hale quoted his opinions so often that it became a family joke to wonder how much time the men spent studying, when so much time was spent in conversation.

One of Margaret's tasks was to find a servant to help Dixon in the kitchen. The rough girls who had replied to their advertisements were not at all suitable, so Margaret went up and down the Milton streets, visiting shops, looking for a girl who Dixon would accept. But all the girls she saw preferred to work at a mill, where the wages were better. In London, when Margaret went out walking, she had always been accompanied by a servant, but here she walked alone, among the crowds who poured in and out of the factories. They came rushing along, with loud voices and fearless faces, and at first they frightened her. The girls commented on her clothes and sometimes even touched them, but they were not unfriendly. The undisguised admiration of the men upset her, however, as she had never received this kind of attention before.

She was returning home one day when a middle-aged worker said as he passed her, 'A face as pretty as yours should always be smiling.' The man looked so weighed down with worries that she smiled at him and he smiled back. Whenever they passed each other again they did not speak, but a silent recognition grew between them. Once or twice she saw him walking with an unhealthy-looking girl, apparently his daughter.

One morning in May, she had been to pick flowers in the countryside and was walking back home when she met the couple. She offered the flowers to the girl, and the girl's pale blue eyes lit up as she took them.

'Thank you, miss, that's kind of you,' said the man. 'You're not from round here, I don't think.'

'No,' said Margaret, half sighing. 'I come from the south.'

The girl was walking very slowly and Margaret turned to her and said sweetly, 'I am afraid you are not very strong.'

'No,' said the girl, 'and I never will be.'

'Spring is here,' said Margaret.

'It won't do me any good.'

'She's right, poor girl,' said the man.

Margaret felt shocked but also interested. 'Where do you live?' she asked.

'9 Frances Street.'

'And your name? I must not forget that.'

'Nicholas Higgins. And she's called Bessy Higgins.'

'I would like to come and see you,' said Margaret shyly.

'I don't like strangers in my house,' said the man but, seeing Margaret's expression, added, 'You may come if you like.'

As the couple turned to go their own way, the girl said, 'You won't forget to come and see us.'

'She'll come, I can see it in her face,' said the father impatiently. 'Come on, Bess. The mill bell is ringing.'

Margaret went home, thinking about her new friends, glad that she had found a human interest; from that day, Milton seemed a brighter place to her.

## Chapter 4  New Friends

The day after Margaret's meeting with Higgins and his daughter, Mr Hale nervously informed his wife and daughter that he had invited Mr Thornton to tea that night.

'Mr Thornton! And tonight! What does the man want to come here for?' Mrs Hale said, with the expression of pain on her face that had recently become habitual.

But since the invitation had been given, preparations had to be made, and Margaret spent the day ironing in the kitchen, while Dixon made cakes.

When Mrs Hale saw her daughter's tired face, she was upset. 'If anyone had told me, when I was Miss Beresford, that a child of mine would have to work in the kitchen like a servant, preparing to entertain a tradesman – '

'Oh, Mother!' said Margaret. 'I don't mind what kind of work I do, if it's for you and Father. And poor Mr Thornton can't help being a tradesman. With his education, I don't suppose he could do anything else.'

In Mr Thornton's house a similar, yet different scene was taking place. A large-boned woman in her late sixties, with strong features and a severe expression, sat sewing in an expensively decorated dining-room. She was busy mending a long tablecloth when her son entered the room.

'John, I thought you were going to tea with that friend of Mr Bell's.'

'I am, Mother. I've come home to change my clothes.'

'Change your clothes! Why should you put on your best clothes to have a cup of tea with an old clergyman?'

'Mr Hale is a gentleman and his wife and daughter are ladies.'

'You have never mentioned his family before.'

'I have only met the daughter – and that was for half an hour.'

'Don't let her try to catch you, John. You're a rich man.'

Mr Thornton frowned. 'Mother, when I met her, she treated me as if she was a queen and I was her servant. You need not worry.' He left the room.

'As if she was a queen and he was her servant!' Mrs Thornton thought aloud. 'Where could a woman find another man like John? He has the best heart I ever knew! I hate her!'

♦

Mr Thornton arrived at the Hales' house at exactly half-past seven. Mr Hale greeted him kindly and introduced him to his wife, whose pale face and tired manner suggested that she was not well. It was getting dark and Margaret was lighting the lamp as he entered. Looking around the sitting-room, the mill owner was impressed by its prettiness and style; somehow, it was much more comfortable and attractive than any of the rooms in his own large house.

Margaret was serving the tea, and her movements were so graceful that at first he could not take his eyes off her. But soon he and Mr Hale began discussing a subject that interested them both – the relationship between the mill owners and the workers. Now it was Margaret's turn to watch Mr Thornton and notice how different he was to her father. While Mr Hale's expression was soft and dreamy, Mr Thornton's eyes seemed to want to enter the heart of everything he looked at. He rarely smiled, but when he did, it had the effect of sudden sunlight. Margaret liked Mr Thornton's smile; it was the first thing she had admired in her father's new friend.

'I won't deny that I am proud of belonging to a manufacturing town,' said Mr Thornton to Mr Hale. 'I would rather be a working man here than a rich man in the south, living a dull, lazy life.'

Hearing this, Margaret felt so angry that her face reddened. 'You do not know anything about the south. There is less trade there but there is also less suffering. I see men in the streets here who work so hard they look ill.'

'And may I say you do not know the north?' said Mr Thornton gently, seeing that he had really hurt Margaret. But she did not answer and so he continued the conversation with Mr Hale.

'At the beginning of this century the mill owners had almost unlimited power. We have much less power now. Now there are more factories, and more men are needed, so the relationship between the mill owners and the workers is more evenly balanced. One cannot say who will win the battle.'

'Must you call it a battle between the two classes?' asked Mr Hale.

'But it is a battle. Those who are successful work harder and behave more wisely than those who are not. And it is an unfortunate truth that lazy and foolish people will always oppose those who are successful.'

'If I understand you correctly, you consider all those who are not successful in the world, for whatever reason, as your enemies, then,' said Margaret, in a clear, cold voice.

'As their own enemies, certainly,' said Mr Thornton, quickly, hurt by the disapproval in her voice. But he felt that he should explain his meaning more clearly. He knew he could best illustrate what he wanted to say by telling them something about his own life. Feeling a little shy, so that his face went slightly red, he continued: 'I say this because of my own experiences. Sixteen years ago my father died in very miserable circumstances. I was taken from school and had to become a man in only a few days. Fortunately, I had a very strong and determined mother. We went to live in a small country town. There I found work in a clothes shop, and the money I earned, which was very little, had to support my mother, my sister and myself. My mother taught me to save a little money each week, and in this way I learnt self-control. Now that I can afford to look after her in the way she deserves, I thank her silently for teaching me this valuable lesson. I believe that unsuccessful people have not bothered to learn it, and so I feel contempt for them.'

Margaret did not reply to this speech and soon Mr Thornton got up to leave. He shook hands with Mr and Mrs Hale, then went towards Margaret to shake hands with her too, as was the custom in Milton. But it was not the custom in the south and Margaret just bowed, although, as soon as she saw the hand half extended, then quickly withdrawn, she was sorry she had not been aware of his intention. Mr Thornton, however, did not realise this, and walked off angrily, telling himself that she was the proudest, most unpleasant girl he had ever met.

'Margaret,' said Mr Hale, after Mr Thornton had left, 'I could not help watching your face when Mr Thornton confessed that he had been a shop boy. I was aware of it because Mr Bell had told me, but I half expected you to get up and leave the room.'

'Oh Father, do you really think I am so silly? I liked the story of his childhood more than anything else he said. Everything else disgusted me – he was so hard! He didn't seem to realise that other people may not have received the training his mother gave him, or that it was his duty to help the less fortunate. But I did like the way he spoke about himself so simply, and with such love and respect for his mother.'

'I heard a lot about his early life from Mr Bell before we came here,' said Mr Hale, 'and as he has told you part of it, I will tell you the rest. His father lost all his money and then killed himself. After his death, no one offered to help the family. Mr Bell said they had very little to eat for years. But when the young man had made enough money, he visited all the people whom his father owed money to and began to pay them back. It was done very quietly, but finally he paid all his father's debts. It helped him that Mr Bell, one of the people his father owed money to, invited him to work with him.'

'That was a very fine thing for Mr Thornton to do,' said Margaret. 'It is such a pity, then, that wealth is the only thing that matters to him.'

She was getting up to leave the room as she said this and, just as she was opening the door, she said, 'Father, I do think that Mr Thornton is a very unusual man. But I don't like him at all.'

'And I do,' said her father, laughing, 'although I don't see him as a hero or anything like that. But goodnight, child. Your mother looks very tired tonight.'

Margaret had noticed her mother's unhealthy appearance in recent weeks and it had made her anxious. Realising from her father's remark that he had noticed it too, she felt even more fearful. There were good reasons to worry about her mother's health. Their life in Milton was so different from the way they had lived in Helstone, where they had spent much of their time outside, in the fresh country air. In Milton the air was heavy with factory smoke and Mrs Hale did not like going out much. And then there were the financial worries and the difficulty in finding a servant. There were other signs that something was wrong. Margaret sometimes heard her mother and Dixon talking in low voices in the bedroom; Dixon would come out crying, which was the way she behaved when Mrs Hale was very upset about something. Margaret suspected that her mother had some secret about her health that she was not telling her.

That night, she lay awake for hours, planning ways in which she could help. If she could find a servant to help Dixon with her duties, then Dixon could give her mother the attention she had been accustomed to all her life.

Margaret spent the next few days looking for a servant, but without success. One afternoon she met Bessy Higgins in the street and stopped to talk to her.

'Bessy, how are you? Better, I hope, now that it's warmer.'

'Better and not better, if you see what I mean.'

'Not exactly,' said Margaret, smiling.

'I'm not coughing, so I'm better in that way. But I'm tired of Milton and I want to go to a better place.'

For a minute or two Margaret did not speak, then she said in a low voice, 'Bessy, do you really wish to die?'

Bessy replied, 'If you'd lived the life I've lived, and been as sick as I have, then you'd be glad enough when the doctor said he feared you'd never see another winter.'

'Why, Bessy? What kind of a life have you had?'

'If you'd come to my house when you said you would, I could maybe have told you.'

'I have been very busy,' said Margaret quietly. 'But may I go home with you now?'

Seeing from Margaret's soft, friendly expression that she was sincere, Bessy said, 'You may come if you want.'

They walked together in silence until they reached a narrow, dirty street. When they entered the house, Margaret saw that a girl, younger than Bessy but taller, was washing clothes in a rough, capable way, making a lot of noise as she did so. Bessy sat down, breathless and exhausted, and closed her eyes. Margaret asked the sister, who was called Mary, to fetch a glass of water, and Bessy drank it and felt better. She asked Margaret where she had lived before Milton, and Margaret described Helstone to her, doing her best to describe its beauty.

'I used to think once that if I could have a day of doing nothing – a day in some quiet place like the one you described – I would feel better,' Bessy said. 'But now I've had so many days of doing nothing, and I'm just as tired as when I was at work. I was well until mother died, but soon after that I got sick. It was when I began to work in a part of the factory where the air was filled with white dust from the cotton. They say the dust gets into your lungs, and you start coughing blood.'

'But can't they do something about it?' asked Margaret, shocked.

'There's a great wheel they can use to blow away the dust, but it costs a lot of money. They didn't have one at our factory.'

'How old are you?' asked Margaret.

'Nineteen in July.'

'And I too am nineteen.' Thinking of the contrast between them, Margaret could not speak for a moment. Then, seeing that Bessy was becoming even more tired, she said, 'I must go. I will come again as soon as I can. But if I don't come for a week or two, don't think I've forgotten you. I may be busy.'

'I know you'll come again. But remember – in a week or two, I may be dead and buried.'

'I'll come as soon as I can,' said Margaret, holding Bessy's hand in hers for a moment.

◆

From that day, Mrs Hale seemed to become more and more unwell. It was about ten months now since Edith's marriage and, looking back, Margaret saw so many difficulties; but there had been moments of real pleasure, and it was a comfort to her that she and her mother were becoming closer at last.

One evening, when Mr Hale was away, Mrs Hale began to talk about Frederick. She explained that he had taken the name of Dickinson so that he would not be recognised. She told

Margaret to go to her desk and open a drawer, where she would find his letters. Margaret carried the yellow, sea-stained letters to her mother, who untied the string that held them together with trembling fingers. She gave them to Margaret to read, and at the same time told her the story of the mutiny, as she had learnt it from Frederick.

Captain Reid, the captain of the *Russell*, Frederick's ship, had been a cruel man who treated his men so badly that one of them had died. The men had mutinied and put Captain Reid off the *Russell*, sending him out in a boat with some of his officers; the boat had been found some days later by a West Indian ship. Frederick, who was one of the most senior officers, had been among those who had mutinied. Reporting the incident, the English newspapers had named him as one of those responsible for the mutiny, and said that he ought to be hung by the neck.

'He fought injustice and I am proud of him,' said Mrs Hale in a weak voice. 'But I wish I could see him once more.'

'It is seven years ago – would they still hang him, Mother?'

'Some of the sailors who mutinied were captured and tried in court. They were hanged. And the worst thing was that the court said that their superior officers had encouraged them to mutiny.'

The two women were silent for a long time.

'And Frederick was in South America for several years?'

'Yes. And now he is in Spain, somewhere near Cadiz. If he comes to England he will be hanged. I shall never see his face again.'

Mrs Hale turned her face to the wall and lay very still; nothing could be said to comfort her. When her father came in, Margaret left the room, seeing no promise of brightness anywhere.

# Chapter 5  A Strike Begins

Four or five days after his visit to the Hales, Mr Thornton decided that his mother and sister should also visit them, but he had some difficulty persuading them to do so. Mrs Thornton did not often go out visiting and she did not understand why she should become friends with a teacher. Eventually she agreed, but it was then Fanny's turn to protest.

'I am not coming,' she said. 'I have a headache today.'

'Fanny! I wish you to go,' said her brother authoritatively. 'Please go without me saying any more about it.'

Mrs Thornton sighed. Unlike her mother and her brother Fanny was not a strong character, and Mrs Thornton had an unconscious contempt for those who were weak. She behaved lovingly towards her daughter and a stranger might have thought that she loved her more than her son. The opposite was true. The honesty with which mother and son spoke to each other showed the great respect they had for each other's strength. Mrs Thornton thanked God for her son every day of her life.

That afternoon, Mrs Thornton and Fanny set out in their carriage for Crampton. When she entered the Hales' little sitting-room, Mrs Thornton, who was shy and hated meeting strangers, hid her shyness by looking even more severe than usual. She and Mrs Hale started a conversation about servants while Margaret, who was sewing, tried hard to talk to Fanny.

'I see no piano, so I suppose you are not musical,' said Fanny.

'I am fond of good music but I cannot play well myself. We sold our old piano when we came here.'

'How can you exist without one? A piano is a necessity!'

'You have good concerts here, I believe,' said Margaret coldly.

'Oh yes! One is sure to hear the newest music here.'

25

'Do you like new music, then?'

'Oh, one knows it is the fashion in London. You have been to London, of course.'

'Yes,' said Margaret. 'I lived there for several years. Have you never been there? It is an easy journey by train.'

'I would love to go, but mother does not wish to. She is very proud of Milton, you see. To me it is a dirty, smoky place, but I believe she admires it for those qualities.'

'If it has been Mrs Thornton's home for some years, I can understand her loving it,' said Margaret in her clear voice.

'May I ask what you are saying about me, Miss Hale?' asked Mrs Thornton.

Fanny replied, 'Oh Mother, we are trying to understand why you are so fond of Milton.'

'Thank you,' said Mrs Thornton. 'I do not feel that my natural liking for the place where I was born requires an explanation.'

Margaret was cross that Fanny had made it seem that they had been criticising her mother; she also disliked the way Mrs Thornton had spoken to her.

After a pause, Mrs Thornton said, 'Do you know anything about Milton, Miss Hale? Have you visited our splendid factories?'

'No,' said Margaret honestly. 'I don't think I would greatly enjoy visiting such places.'

'No doubt,' said Mrs Thornton, sounding displeased. 'I thought that as newcomers to a manufacturing town, you might have been interested in finding out more about its business.'

Soon after this, the visit ended. 'Fanny,' said her mother as they drove away, 'we will be polite to these Hales, but don't become friendly with the daughter. She will do you no good. The mother looks very ill and seems a nice, quiet kind of person. Well, I suppose John will be satisfied now.'

♦

The next day, Mr Hale and Margaret returned Mrs Thornton's visit. To their surprise, they discovered that the Thorntons lived next to their mill in Marlborough Street. Behind a long wall there was a large yard, with offices on one side and the mill on the other. At the end of the yard was a tall, attractive house. They knocked at the door and were taken upstairs to a large sitting-room. Mrs Thornton entered a few minutes later.

'How is Mr Thornton?' asked Mr Hale. 'He was unable to come for his lesson yesterday and I was afraid he was not well.'

'My son is rarely ill. He told me he was too busy to visit you last night. But I know he values the hours he spends with you.'

'I find them equally pleasant,' said Mr Hale. 'He has such an appreciation of Ancient Greek literature.'

'I have no doubt that to know Ancient Greek is desirable for those who do not work. But I advised my son not to study it. His work requires all his attention. It ought to be enough for him to have one great desire and to aim only at that.'

'And that is – ?' asked Mr Hale.

Mrs Thornton blushed as she answered, 'To have a high position among the manufacturers in this country. My son has earned this place for himself. All over Europe, the name of John Thornton of Milton is respected among businessmen.'

Both Mr Hale and Margaret felt uncomfortably aware that they had never heard of this great name until Mr Bell had told them about him. The expression on Margaret's face revealed this to the sensitive Mrs Thornton.

'You are thinking you have never heard of this wonderful son of mine, Miss Hale.'

'Yes, it is true. But since I have been here I have heard enough to make me respect and admire him.'

Mrs Thornton smiled, but said, 'Thank you, Miss Hale. Many young women would not have said that, fearing that it would seem that they had plans to win my son's heart.'

On hearing this, Margaret laughed, but stopped when she saw Mrs Thornton's annoyed look.

'I'm sorry, madam. But I really am not interested in that way,' she said.

'Young ladies have been, before now,' said Mrs Thornton stiffly.

'I hope I will see Mr Thornton on Thursday,' said Mr Hale, trying to change the subject.

'I cannot say. There will almost certainly be a strike.'

'A strike! Why?' asked Margaret.

'The workers want higher wages, I suppose,' said Mr Hale.

'That is what they say, but the truth is, they want to be more powerful than the mill owners. They strike every five or six years. But I believe that if the men do strike, the mill owners have some ideas that will teach them not do it again in a hurry.'

♦

That evening Mr Thornton came to see Mr Hale. He was shown into the sitting-room, where Margaret was reading aloud to her father and mother.

'I have come partly to bring a note from my mother and partly to apologise for not coming for my lesson yesterday. The note contains the address you asked for.'

'Thank you,' said Margaret quickly, holding out her hand to take the note. She did not want her mother to know that her father, who was becoming worried about his wife's health, had asked Mr Thornton to give them the name of a good doctor. Mr Thornton seemed to understand immediately and gave her the note without another word of explanation.

Mr Hale began to talk about the strike. Mr Thornton, looking angry, said, 'Yes, the fools are going to strike. They think the cotton trade is as good as it was last year. They want better pay, but because we won't explain why we have refused

28

their demand, and tell them we may have to lower wages, they think we are trying to cheat them.'

'But why can't you explain your reasons?' asked Margaret.

'Do you give your servants reasons for the way in which you spend your money? We manufacturers have a right to choose what we do with it.'

'What about the rights of the workers?' said Margaret quietly.

'I'm sorry, I did not hear what you said.'

'I would rather not repeat it,' she said. 'I don't think you will understand.'

'Please try and explain,' said Mr Thornton, who really wanted to know what she had said.

'I meant that the workers have rights too. Surely they deserve to know why you cannot pay them more.'

Mr Thornton paused for a moment and then said, 'In my opinion, the workers are like children. I do not think we mill owners try to keep them like that – it is just the way they are. They need to be told what to do and, like children, they do not need to be given reasons why.'

Margaret replied, 'I very much disagree with you. There should be friendship and cooperation between the manufacturers and their workers. We all depend on each other.'

The conversation continued with neither side willing to change their position. Mr Thornton got up to go. Margaret smiled at him but did not put out her hand, and again, as he left, he told himself that she was unpleasantly proud.

That night, as the Thorntons sat in their sitting-room, Mrs Thornton asked her son what he had done that day. On hearing that he had visited the Hales, Fanny said, 'Are they really so different to most people one meets?'

Her words annoyed her brother, but he did not reply.

'They do not seem unusual to me,' said Mrs Thornton.

'He appears a good kind of man – not clever enough to be in trade. The wife sees herself as a lady. The girl is the one who puzzles me. She seems to have great self-importance and I can't understand why. They're not rich and, from what I understand, they never have been.'

'And she can't even play the piano, Mother,' said Fanny.

'Go on, Fanny. What else does she need to bring her up to your standard?' said Mr Thornton, who was walking up and down the sitting-room. Then he stopped and said bravely, 'Mother, I want you to like Miss Hale.'

'Why?' she asked, surprised. 'You're not thinking of marrying her – a girl without any money?'

'She would never have me,' he answered with a short laugh.

'From what she told me, I don't think she would,' said his mother. 'Her opinion of herself is far too high to think of you!'

If these words hurt her son, the fading evening light hid the expression on his face, and in a minute he said cheerfully, 'Well, I'm sure of that too, and have no intention of asking her to be my wife. But I see trouble for that girl – her mother is very ill – and I would like you to be a friend to her, in case she needs one.'

'I cannot forgive her pride,' said his mother, 'but because you ask me, John, I will be her friend, if she needs it.'

'I am so tired of this subject,' said Fanny.

'Well,' said her brother rather bitterly, 'shall we talk about the strike then? The men at Hamper's mill are going to strike tomorrow. Mine will strike next week.'

'You are going to have difficulty completing your business orders,' said Mrs Thornton, looking worried. 'Can you get workers from Ireland?'

'Yes, I can, and I will if the strike goes on too long. But it will make our workers very angry.'

He continued walking up and down the room, not speaking but taking deep breaths from time to time. Fanny started chatting to her mother and at ten o'clock the family said good night. Mr Thornton remained in the room, anxiously considering his position. Because of the strike, all his business plans were in confusion; the workers seemed to him to be completely mad.

'I can give them a fortnight – no more. If they haven't understood the situation by then, I'll be forced to get workers from Ireland,' he thought.

♦

In the second week of the strike, Margaret went to visit Bessy. When she arrived, Nicholas Higgins and his daughter were sitting by the fire. Nicholas, who was smoking a pipe, stood up, pushing his chair towards Margaret. She sat down and enquired about Bessy's health.

'She's upset about the strike. She doesn't like it.'

'This is the third strike I've seen,' said Bessy, sighing.

'We'll win this time, you can be sure of that,' said Nicholas.

'Why are you striking?' asked Margaret.

'There are five or six mill owners who want to pay us less than we get now,' replied Nicholas. 'And we won't agree. We'll die first. But don't think I'm striking just for myself. There are only three in my family, but John Boucher next door has a sick wife and six children. He can't manage with the wages he has now from the mill – how is he going to live on less?'

'Perhaps you should ask the mill owners why they want to pay less. The reason may be that business is not good.'

'I don't believe that,' said Nicholas angrily. 'The mill owners will say anything. They use us so that they can get rich. But this time they'll have to give in. They've got a lot of business orders and they need us to do the work.'

Bessy sighed heavily when she heard this and Margaret said, 'You don't like all this struggling and fighting, do you?'

'No,' said Bessy, 'I'm tired of it all – all this shouting and talk of work and wages. Oh! The tobacco smoke makes me feel ill!'

'Then I'll never smoke in the house again,' said her father gently. 'But why didn't you tell me before?'

Receiving no answer, he went outside to finish his pipe, and Bessy said in a low voice, 'He needs his pipe. It's one of the few comforts he has – his work is so hard and boring. And when a strike begins, everyone's so hopeful at first. And then it goes on and on and people get angry and depressed.'

'Maybe you're exaggerating because you're not well,' said Margaret.

'No, I'm not exaggerating. People have been coming to see us and they all say how much they hate the mill owners. I've seen women crying because they have no money to buy food and their children are so hungry they can't sleep at night.'

'You're looking more and more feverish, Bessy. And your hand is so hot!' Margaret found some water, wet her handkerchief and laid it on Bessy's forehead. 'I must go,' she said, 'but I'll come back soon.'

'You're not like anyone I've ever known. I don't know what to think of you.'

'I don't know what to think of myself. Goodbye.'

Bessy watched her as she walked out of the house. 'I wonder if there are many people like her, down south. She's so strong and bright! But will she stay like that, I wonder?'


## Chapter 6  The Shadow of Death

Dr Donaldson, the doctor recommended by Mr Thornton, came to call on Mrs Hale soon after Margaret's visit to Bessy. Margaret was not allowed into the room while he was there, but Dixon was, and this made her feel very jealous.

She waited anxiously outside, and when the doctor came out,

she said quickly, 'My father is out. Would you come downstairs?'

Dr Donaldson followed her into Mr Hale's study.

'What is the matter with Mother?' Margaret asked.

The doctor hesitated and she said, 'If the news is bad, my father must be told the news gently. Only I can do this.'

'My dear, your mother said that you must not be told.'

'I feel sure that you have not promised to keep the secret.'

'Well,' said the doctor, smiling sadly, 'you are right. I did not promise. In fact, I'm afraid you will all know soon enough.'

Margaret went very white, but no part of her face moved. Dr Donaldson was a man who understood people well and he saw immediately that she was strong enough to be told the truth. He spoke two sentences in a low voice, watching her all the time.

Her eyes grew wide and she went even whiter. Then she said, 'I have been afraid of this for many weeks.' She began to cry, but a few moments later, the tears stopped. 'Will my mother suffer much?' she asked.

He shook his head. 'I can't say. But the latest discoveries of medical science can help a lot.'

'My father!' she said, trembling all over. 'He must not be told the truth yet – not all at once. It would kill him!'

'I do not know Mr Hale, so it is difficult to give advice. But I will visit often and your father will be a little more prepared for the truth. And when I come again, it will be as a friend.'

Margaret was crying so much that she could not speak, but she shook the doctor's hand as he left.

'That's a fine girl,' thought Dr Donaldson, as he sat in his carriage. 'What a queen she is! The way she threw her head back, forcing me to tell her the truth. If I were thirty years younger, I would have fallen in love with her.'

Meanwhile Margaret sat in her father's study, trying to find some strength. After some minutes she ran upstairs. Her mother was lying in an armchair, looking quite peaceful.

'Margaret, how strange you look! What is the matter?' Suddenly guessing the truth, Mrs Hale said, 'Dr Donaldson hasn't been talking to you, has he, child?'

'Oh yes, Mother, he did. I made him.' Margaret knelt by her mother's side and started to cry and kiss her hand. 'Oh Mother, let me be your nurse. It will be such a comfort to me.'

'My poor child! Dixon and I thought you should not know.'

'Dixon thought!' said Margaret scornfully. 'I am your daughter, Mother! I only want to be near you. In Harley Street, I used to cry in bed at night, thinking you would forget me.'

'And I used to wonder, what will Margaret think of our little cottage after her luxurious life with Aunt Shaw?'

'Oh Mother, how can you say that? I loved Helstone so much!'

'I shall never see Helstone again. But Margaret – Frederick!' Mrs Hale started sobbing. 'Frederick, Frederick, come to me! I am dying, come to me!'

Dixon came running in, and they lifted Mrs Hale into her bed. Margaret sat with her until she fell asleep, then the two women went into the sitting-room to talk.

'Look what you've done to your mother – and now I suppose you'll tell your father,' Dixon said angrily.

'No, Dixon,' said Margaret sorrowfully, 'I won't tell him. He would be too upset.' And she burst into tears.

'Miss Margaret, my dear, I've had to keep this secret for so long and your mother's the person I love most in the world.'

'Oh, Dixon!' said Margaret. 'I've been cross with you so often, not realising what a terrible burden you were carrying!'

'You dear child! Now you go out for a long walk and you'll feel better. I'll look after your mother.'

'I will.' Margaret gave Dixon a kiss and left the room.

Dixon watched her as she walked down the street. 'She's as sweet as a nut, that girl. There are three people I love – her mother, Frederick and her. Her father's always been too busy thinking and reading to look after my lady properly. And look what's happened to him! Poor child! Her clothes look old. In Helstone she didn't need to mend her socks or clean her gloves. And now – !'

When Mr Hale came home several hours later, he enquired anxiously about Dr Donaldson's visit. Margaret told him that the doctor did not think her mother was seriously ill at present but that he felt she needed care; he had given her some medicine and would visit frequently. Mr Hale's nervous reaction showed that he realised that his wife might be in danger. All that evening he kept going into his wife's bedroom to see if she was still asleep. Finally he came back looking comforted.

'She's awake now, Margaret. She has asked for a cup of tea.'

♦

During the next week, Mrs Hale's health improved and the family began to hope that she would recover. But in the streets outside there was an atmosphere of gloom and discontent. Mr Hale knew several workers and was depressed by their stories of hunger and suffering. When Mr Thornton next came to visit, Mr Hale told him these stories. The mill owner explained that in business, profits depended to some extent on the country's economy. When times were difficult, some manufacturers would lose their businesses and their workers would lose their jobs as a result. He spoke without emotion, seeming to feel that neither the employer nor the workers had a right to complain.

Mr Thornton's coldness shocked Margaret. How could he talk as if trade was the only thing that mattered? When he had arrived that afternoon, he had offered to help her mother in any way he could. Margaret could not understand how those eyes, which were so kind when he talked about her mother, could belong to the same man who spoke about his workers so pitilessly.

Later that week Margaret visited Bessy, who seemed even more exhausted than usual. The girl told her a sad story about the Boucher family next door. John Boucher, one of the strikers, had suddenly died three days ago. But this was not all. Mrs Boucher was becoming more and more unwell and the youngest child was so weak with hunger that he was likely to die. The story shocked Margaret and she immediately took out her purse and pressed the money in it into Bessy's hand. When she returned home, she told her parents about the family, and the next day a big basket of food was sent to them.

That evening, Margaret and her father went for a long walk and, as they returned home, began to discuss Mr Thornton.

'He must know how much his workers hate him,' said Margaret. 'They think he has no feelings.'

'I disagree. In my opinion, he is a passionate man but is too proud to show his emotions.'

'I am not sure. But he is very clever and has great strength of character, and I am starting to like him a little.'

By now they were at their front door. Dixon opened it and when they saw her face they both started to tremble.

'Thank God you've come! Dr Donaldson is here. She's better now, but I thought she was going to die an hour ago!'

Mr Hale took Margaret's arm to prevent himself from falling.

'Oh, I should not have left her!' cried Margaret.

Dr Donaldson met them inside. 'She is better for the moment,' he whispered.

'For the moment! Let me go to her!' cried Mr Hale.

They entered the bedroom. Mrs Hale lay on the bed, and from the look on her face it was clear to them all that death was near. Mr Hale began to shake and Dr Donaldson took him downstairs and helped him into a chair.

After some moments, Mr Hale said, making a great effort, 'Margaret, did you know about this? It was cruel of you.'

'I told her not to tell you,' said Dr Donaldson. 'Your wife will sleep well tonight and will be better tomorrow, I hope.'

'But what about the illness? Please tell me the truth.'

'We cannot stop it, only delay it.' Dr Donaldson explained that they need not fear that Mrs Hale would die immediately, but that she would not recover. He left, promising to return early in the morning.

Both Mr Hale and Dixon did not sleep for many hours. Margaret felt as if she would never sleep again. To the young woman watching by her mother's bed, her life until that moment seemed unreal. Life seemed so shadowy, and passed so quickly! When the morning came, cold and grey, it seemed as if the terrible night was also a dream; it too was past.

When Mrs Hale woke the next morning, she was unaware of how ill she had been, and was rather surprised by Dr Donaldson's early visit and by the anxious faces of her husband and child. The doctor allowed her to return to the sitting-room, but she was uncomfortable in every position and that night she became very feverish. The doctor thought that a water-bed might help and suggested that the family could borrow one from the Thorntons', since he knew they had one.

'I could go and ask them to lend it to us while mother is asleep,' said Margaret.

That afternoon Mrs Hale seemed much better, and Margaret left the house and set off for the Thorntons'.


## Chapter 7  Dangerous Times

It was about two miles from Crampton to Marlborough Street. Margaret, who was absorbed in her own thoughts, did not notice anything unusual for the first mile and a half of her journey. But then she realised that there were even more people than usual

37

on the crowded roads and that they were not moving forward but were talking excitedly.

It was only when she arrived in Marlborough Street that she realised that there was an atmosphere of real anger in the crowd and that in the distance the low roar of hundreds of voices could be heard. Margaret noticed all this but did not understand its meaning. There was only one thought in her mind; her mother was going to die.

When she arrived at the house, the man who guarded the wall's tall wooden gates would only open them a little way, but when he recognised her, he let her in and quickly locked the gates behind her.

Margaret walked up to the door of the house and was shown into the sitting-room. Unusually, there was no sound of machinery from the factory, but the shouts of the crowds were growing louder.

Fanny entered and said, 'Mother will be here soon. My brother has brought in workers from Ireland and the Milton people are very angry. For their own safety, the Irish workers are in the top room of the mill.'

Mrs Thornton came in, looking thunderous, and Margaret realised she had arrived at a bad time; nevertheless, she explained her mother's situation and made her request. Mrs Thornton, who was listening to the shouts of the crowd outside, did not reply. Then she jumped up and exclaimed, 'They're at the gates! Call John, Fanny! They'll break the gates down!'

The women and the servants ran to the windows to look out. The wooden gates were shaking as men threw themselves against them. Fanny screamed, while Mrs Thornton's face was white with fear. Mr Thornton appeared; his face was a little red but he did not look at all frightened.

'You have come at an unfortunate moment, Miss Hale,' he said. 'Mother, you and the servants will be safer upstairs.'

The servants ran upstairs, but Mrs Thornton said, 'I will stay with you, of course. When will the soldiers arrive?'

'In about twenty minutes,' said her son calmly.

'Twenty minutes!' cried Mrs Thornton, looking very frightened.

Mr Thornton went to the windows to close them, and as he did so they heard the sound of the gates breaking open. Fanny fainted and her mother ran to her and carried her upstairs.

'Should you not go upstairs too, Miss Hale?' said Mr Thornton.

'No,' said Margaret, but now the workers had arrived at the house and were shouting so loudly that he could not hear her.

'Let them shout!' said Mr Thornton coolly. 'The soldiers will be here soon. Be brave, Miss Hale.'

'Don't be afraid for me. But please don't let the soldiers cut down those poor men,' said Margaret passionately. 'They are human beings. Go out and speak to them, man to man!'

A dark cloud came over Mr Thornton's face when she said this, and he was silent. Then, 'I will go,' he said.

He left the room. Margaret ran to the window and soon saw that he was standing on the steps to the house with his arms folded. As she watched, she saw some of the younger men in the crowd take off their shoes to throw at him.

She ran downstairs and opened the door. Placing herself in front of Mr Thornton, she cried, 'Do not use violence! The soldiers are coming – go before it is too late!'

Mr Thornton moved to one side, so that he could be seen.

'Send the Irish workers away!' shouted an angry voice.

'No!' exclaimed Mr Thornton, and the crowd started shouting insults. Margaret saw that the group of younger men were aiming their shoes at him. Desperately trying to save him, she stood in front of him and threw her arms around him.

'Go away!' he said, and shook her off.

At that moment, a shoe almost hit them. A second later, a stone hit Margaret hard on the forehead and she fell onto Mr Thornton's shoulder. He put his arms around her.

'How brave you are!' he said scornfully to the crowds. 'Hundreds of you attacking one woman.'

The crowd went silent. Then, slowly, people started moving towards the gates. Only one voice cried, 'The stone was meant for you, but you were hiding behind a woman!'

Shaking with anger, Mr Thornton placed Margaret gently on the steps and walked right into the middle of the crowd.

'Kill me, if that is what you want,' he said, but the crowd continued moving towards the gates.

When he was sure they would not turn back, Mr Thornton ran back up the steps to Margaret.

'I'm all right,' she said, and fainted.

He picked her up and carried her, still unconscious, into the dining-room. There, he laid her on the sofa and cried passionately, 'Oh, Margaret! No one knows what you mean to me! You are the only woman I have ever loved!'

His mother appeared; fortunately, she did not seem to have heard his words. He told her what had happened and asked her to look after Margaret while he went to talk to the Irish workers. A servant called Jane came and started to bathe Margaret's face. Margaret opened her eyes but after some moments closed them again.

'We must fetch a doctor,' said Mrs Thornton, but she could not persuade either Fanny or the servants to go. Finally, she said angrily, 'I will go myself,' and left the room.

Jane, who had seen everything from an upstairs window, told Fanny what had happened.

'She had her arms around Mr Thornton's neck,' said Jane.

'I don't believe it,' said Fanny. 'I know she cares for my brother – anyone can see that. And I'm sure she would love it if he married her – which he never will! But I don't believe she would actually throw her arms around him!'

'Well, she did,' replied Jane.

As she spoke, Margaret's eyes opened and tears started pouring down her face. Mrs Thornton came in, accompanied by a doctor.

'How is she? Are you better, my dear?' she asked.

Margaret gazed dreamily at her. The doctor examined her and then put a small bandage on her forehead. She sat up slowly and said, 'I am better now. I must go home. The bandage is under my hair, so Mother will not see it.'

'You are not well enough to go home,' said Mrs Thornton.

'I must,' said Margaret. 'May I ask for a carriage, please?'

They could not persuade her to stay, and as the doctor did not think that her injuries were serious, it was agreed that she could go but that the doctor would accompany her home.

Five minutes after Margaret left, Mr Thornton came in. 'Where is Miss Hale?' he asked anxiously.

'Gone home,' said his mother. 'She was a lot better.'

'She could not have been well enough.'

'She said she was, and the doctor said she was. She went home in a carriage. Let us talk of something else. She has caused enough disturbance.'

'I don't know what would have happened to me without her.'

'Do you really need a girl to defend you?' asked Mrs Thornton scornfully.

His face turned red. 'Not many girls would have done what she did.'

'A girl in love will do almost anything,' replied his mother, watching him carefully.

'Mother!' He stepped forward, breathing heavily.

Feeling uncomfortable, Mrs Thornton changed the subject. 'You don't think there will be any more violence, do you?'

'The soldiers will make sure there isn't. I'm going to arrange to have a guard around the house and mill.'

He left to do this and returned some hours later, explaining that he had arranged for the leaders of the strike to be arrested. Then he said, 'Mother, I am going to Crampton tomorrow to see Miss Hale.'

'The servant who is taking the water-bed can ask how she is.'

'I want to thank her myself for what she did. But there is another reason why I am going.'

Mrs Thornton knew immediately what he was going to say. 'You feel that because she allowed her feelings about you to overcome her that you must ask her to marry you?'

'I dare not hope she will accept. I cannot believe such a creature cares for me.'

'Don't be foolish, John. You talk as if she were a princess! She has shown her real feelings at last. I admit, I like her more now.'

'Dearest Mother! I feel sure she does not care for me – but I have to ask her.'

They wished each other goodnight and she kissed him, then went upstairs to her bedroom. There she locked the door and burst into tears, unable to bear the idea of losing him.

♦

When Margaret returned home, her father and mother were talking in low voices together, looking very pale.

'Mrs Thornton will send the water-bed, Mother,' said Margaret, still feeling as if she might faint.

'Dear, how tired you look! Is it very hot outside?'

'Yes, and the strikers are very noisy.'

She prepared the tea with trembling hands and was glad that her parents did not notice. It was only when she was alone in her bedroom that she was able to think about the day's events. She sat in her chair and put her hands round her knees.

'I, who despise people who lack self-control, threw my arms around Mr Thornton like a romantic fool! Did I do any good? The crowd would probably have gone away without me.'

This was her first judgement, but when she thought about it more coolly she decided that her actions had probably helped the situation. 'But what made me defend him as if he were a helpless child? I'm not surprised Fanny thought I was in love with him – me, in love with Mr Thornton!' Her pale cheeks became bright red and she started to cry.

'How terrible that they think that about me when I don't care about him at all! But it wasn't fair, one man against so many. I had to help him. I would do the same again if it was necessary.'

Having decided this, she lay down in her bed, too tired to move even one finger. She did not know if she slept that night; in her thoughts, her dreams, people were watching her and discussing her and she was filled with shame.

♦

The next morning was a beautiful day and Margaret decided that she would try to forget all about what had happened. She was doing some sewing in her room when Dixon came to tell her that Mr Thornton had called and wanted to see her.

'I will come,' said Margaret quietly, but it was some minutes before she found the courage to meet him.

Mr Thornton was standing by the sitting-room window, his heart beating fast. When he thought of the touch of Margaret's arms around his neck, he felt as if he were on fire. He was afraid he would lose all self-control, that he would hold out his arms to her and beg her to come into them. He feared that she would reject him, but he could not imagine a future without her.

She came in, looking pale and tired but very beautiful. Mr Thornton went to the door and shut it. He said, 'Miss Hale, I am so very grateful to you for – '

'You had nothing to be grateful for,' said Margaret quickly. 'It was a natural reaction. Any woman would have done the same.'

'I disagree. I owe my life to you. Oh, Miss Hale, I owe everything to you – to the woman I love as I have never loved a woman before.'

He took her hand and held it tight, but she said icily, 'The way you speak shocks me. You seem to think that what I did was because of my feelings for you. You are wrong. I would have done the same for any man in that crowd.'

'Am I not allowed to thank you, or express my feelings?' said Mr Thornton.

'Not in the way you have done.'

'I understand now. It is clear you despise me. I think you do not understand me.'

'I do not wish to understand you.'

'No, I see that you do not.'

Despite his angry words, all Mr Thornton wanted to do was to throw himself at Margaret's feet. She started to cry. He waited, hoping for a reply, but when she remained silent, he picked up his hat to leave.

'You seem insulted by my feelings, but I cannot help it. Until now, I have never loved any woman. I have been too busy. You cannot stop me from loving you, but do not be afraid that I will annoy you by talking about my feelings.'

'I am not afraid,' said Margaret, standing very straight. 'But Mr Thornton, you have been very kind to my father. Please, let us not be angry with each other. Please.'

Her whole manner softened when she said these words, but Mr Thornton did not answer. He refused the hand that she held out, then turned and left the room. Margaret thought she saw tears in his eyes and she felt sorry that she had hurt him. 'But how could I help it?' she asked herself. 'I never liked him. I was polite, but nothing more. This is his fault, not mine.'

♦

When Mr Thornton left the house that morning, he had a violent headache and wanted to sit down and cry, like a little child. A bus stopped and without thinking he got onto it; it took him to a small country town. He went into the fields and walked aimlessly, recalling everything Margaret had said and done that morning. Then he thought about every time he had met her, and the way she had looked and acted. He became more and more certain that there never was and never would be anyone like her. He knew that she did not love him and never would, but he also knew that nothing could stop him from loving her.

He returned to the mill late in the afternoon and spent the rest of the day working; due to the events of the previous day, he had many arrangements to make. It was dark when he returned home, but his mother was waiting for him. She did not want to appear anxious, and when she heard him at the door she pretended to be absorbed in a book.

He came in and at first she did not look up. Then she said, 'Well, John?'

He kissed her on the forehead, and said in a low voice, 'No one loves me – no one cares for me except you, Mother.'

Tears came to his eyes and he turned away and leaned against the wall. She stood up and almost fell. Then, putting her hands on his shoulders, she looked into his eyes and said, 'A mother's love is forever. A girl's love changes with every wind. She would not have you, would she, John?'

'I am not good enough for her, mother. I knew I was not. But I love her more than ever.'

'And I hate her for what she has done to you,' said Mrs Thornton fiercely.

'That is unfair. But let us never talk about her again.'

'With all my heart.'

# Chapter 8  A Time of Change

Margaret was so surprised by Mr Thornton's declaration of love that she remained standing in the middle of the sitting-room for some time after he had gone. She could not help comparing Mr Thornton with Mr Lennox and thinking how different they were. Henry Lennox seemed to have slipped over the boundary between friendship and love for a moment, and to have regretted it almost immediately. With Mr Thornton, on the other hand, there had been no friendship; they had done nothing except argue with one another. And now he had come in this strange, wild way to tell her that he loved her and would always love her! Margaret was horrified by this declaration, but she could not stop thinking about him and the look in his deep, strangely passionate eyes.

Not wanting to be alone, she went upstairs to see her mother, who was resting in her room. Mrs Hale spent five minutes praising the water-bed, which she said was very comfortable, and then turned the conversation to the subject closest to her heart.

'Margaret,' she said, sitting up very straight on her sofa, 'if I am going to die soon, I must see Frederick first. I beg you to bring him to me. If he came for five minutes only, it would not be dangerous! Oh, let me see him before I die!'

Margaret felt that her mother's desire to see Frederick was so natural that she should do everything she could to bring him to her, even though it might be dangerous for Frederick.

'I will write to him tonight. I am sure he will come.'

'You must write this afternoon. The post goes at five. I have so little time left; if we miss one post, it may be too late.'

'But I need to talk to Father and he is out.'

'Do you think he will deny my last wish? I would not be dying if he had not brought me to this smoky, sunless place.'

'Oh, Mother!' said Margaret sadly.

'It is true – he has said so himself. He would do anything for me. Don't lose time, dear Margaret. Write now!'

Margaret sat down to write the letter. She took it to the post office and was walking back home when she met her father.

When he heard what she had done, he looked very worried.

'You should have waited until I came, Margaret,' he said.

'I tried to persuade her.'

'I don't know. If she wants to see him so much, then Frederick must come – it would do her more good than any medicine. But the danger to Frederick is very great, I'm afraid.'

'It is a long time since the mutiny, Father.'

'When a man has been involved in a mutiny, the government never forgets. They will do anything to find him.'

'Oh! What have I done? But it seemed so right at the time.'

'No, I am glad you sent the letter,' Mr Hale said, trying to sound cheerful, but Margaret could see from his face that he was very anxious. They walked home without saying another word.

♦

The next day, Mr Thornton, who was a magistrate, had a meeting with the other Milton magistrates about the riot at his mill two days earlier. Many of these men were older and wealthier than he was, but they listened to his opinions with great respect.

When he left the meeting, Mr Thornton's mind was clear, but within minutes he began to think about Margaret and to remember the feeling of her arms around him. He was walking back to the mill when he met Dr Donaldson, who told him the sad news about Mrs Hale. Mr Thornton asked if he could do anything to help, and when he was told that Mrs Hale often asked for fruit, he went immediately to the best shop in Milton and chose the finest fruit there. It was placed in a basket and he carried it himself, walking fast, to the Hales' house.

The family were in the sitting-room, and he entered, his

eyes shining with kindness, and presented the fruit to Mrs Hale. Margaret, who was sewing, was afraid of making any movement that would make him aware of her presence.

'I'm afraid I cannot stay,' Mr Thornton said. 'But you must allow me the pleasure of bringing some fruit again. Good afternoon, Mr Hale. Goodbye, madam.'

He was gone. Not one word, one glance at Margaret. She thought that he had not seen her.

'How kind of him to think of me,' said Mrs Hale. 'Do you not think so, Margaret?'

'Yes,' said Margaret quietly.

After a few minutes she left the room and met Dixon, who handed her a note.

'That young woman you go to see – Higgins, I mean. She died this morning. Her sister is here and wants to speak to you.'

'Oh, poor Bessy,' said Margaret, bursting into tears, and she went down to the kitchen to see Mary. The girl, who had been crying so much that her face was swollen, explained that that morning, about an hour after Nicholas had gone out, Bessy had suddenly become very ill. Some neighbours had run to Mary's workplace to find her, but they had been unable to find her father. Mary had arrived only a few minutes before Bessy died.

'She loved you so much. Please come and see her, madam. She would have wanted you to.'

'Yes, I will. I'll come this afternoon.'

That afternoon Margaret walked quickly to the Higgins'. Mary opened the door to her and they went upstairs to the room where Bessy lay. Her face, which had often looked so exhausted from pain, now had a soft smile, and although there were tears in Margaret's eyes, deep inside she felt very calm. So this was death! It looked more peaceful than life. Slowly, she turned away from the bed and she and Mary went downstairs without a word.

Nicholas Higgins was standing in the middle of the room. He had only just learnt the news and his eyes were huge and dry and fierce. Margaret tried to creep past him, to leave him with his daughter, but he seized her arm and cried, 'Did you see her die?'

'No,' answered Margaret, standing still.

'You're sure she's dead?'

'She is dead.'

He looked at her searchingly, then suddenly threw himself halfway across the table and began to sob.

'Get out of here!' he cried to Margaret.

She took his hand and held it in hers. It was a long time before he was able to calm down, but then he asked her to come with him to Bessy's room and she did so.

'Nothing can hurt her now,' he said, as he stood by his daughter's bed. He looked so pale and ill that Margaret had the idea of suggesting that he should talk to her father. Higgins desperately needed comfort and, knowing that Mr Hale had been a clergyman, agreed to visit him. Some neighbours came in to look after Mary and the two walked in silence to Crampton. Margaret quickly explained the situation to Mr Hale, and then led Higgins into the study. She went upstairs to see her mother and it was some time before she came down again. She was surprised to see the two men with their heads close together, apparently having a serious conversation. They looked up when Margaret came in and Higgins said proudly, 'We've been discussing religion and now we're talking about the strike.'

'I wish some of the mill owners would meet some of you men and have a good talk about things,' said Mr Hale. 'I am sure it would be the best way of overcoming your difficulties. I wonder if Mr Thornton could be persuaded to do so?'

'Thornton! He's the fellow who brought over the Irish workers! Then the leaders of the riot ruined it for everyone. Violence isn't the way. But now, when people would have thanked him for taking the riot leaders to court, Mr Thornton has decided not to do it. He says they won't be able to find work again, and that's enough punishment.'

'Has the strike ended, then?' asked Margaret.

'Yes,' said Nicholas angrily. 'The mill doors will open again tomorrow.'

'Will you get your old job back?'

'No chance. Hamper, my mill owner, thinks I'm a troublemaker. He'd rather cut his leg off than give my job back to me.'

Margaret thought for a moment, and then said hesitantly, 'Why don't you go to Marlborough Mill and ask Mr Thornton?'

Nicholas shook his head in disbelief. 'Mr Thornton? He won't see me!'

'I will write a note for you to give him,' said Mr Hale, eager to help.

'It's kind of you but I'll do it by myself or not at all. I'll go because you ask me, Miss Margaret. I'll wait for him tomorrow until he comes out of the mill. I'll tell him about the Boucher family and their troubles and that I want to help them. But the clock is striking ten. I must go.'

He rose, looked steadily at Margaret and Mr Hale, brushed his hand across his eyes and left the room.

'How proud that man is!' said Mr Hale, a little annoyed that Higgins had refused his offer of help.

'Yes, but how strong and honest he is, too,' said Margaret.

♦

The next morning, a letter arrived from Edith. It was full of affection, like its writer, and described Edith's little boy, who had been born a few weeks earlier. Edith was very insistent that Margaret and her mother should come and stay with her in Corfu for at least three months; she did not ask Mr Hale, whom she blamed for taking the family away from Helstone.

Margaret would have loved to go to Corfu and live Edith's life, just for one day. She was not yet twenty but she felt so old, and she thought that it might make her feel young again. Her mother came in and they were laughing about Edith's letter when Mr Thornton appeared, with another basket of fruit for Mrs Hale.

He had come because of his great need to see Margaret again, but after he had glanced in her direction, he bowed coldly to her and turned away. He presented the fruit to Mrs Hale and talked kindly to her for a few minutes. He did not look at Margaret and, when she spoke, seemed not to hear her, although his next remark showed that he had. His behaviour was not polite at all, but it was clear to Margaret that the reason why he was behaving badly was because he was very hurt.

He left with one last cold, offended look at her, unaware that his behaviour was making Margaret think about him more than ever before. She regretted hurting him so deeply, and would have been very happy to return to their previous relationship; she now realised that they had in fact been friends.

Mr Thornton, as he walked downstairs, was proud of the way he had forced himself to see her and not reveal his feelings. He thought that he hated seeing the woman who had treated him so cruelly the previous day, but he was very wrong.

## Chapter 9  Mrs Hale

Mrs Thornton came to see Mrs Hale the next morning. Mrs Hale was much worse. A sudden change had taken place during the night, and now, with her grey face and hollow cheeks, she looked as if death could not be far away. Mrs Thornton had not believed that Mrs Hale was really ill, and she had only come because her son had insisted, but now that the reality of the

51

younger woman's death was clear, she softened immediately.

Mrs Hale lay still, then with a great effort reached for her visitor's hand and whispered, 'My child will be without a mother – in a strange place. If I die – will you – '

'You wish me to be your daughter's friend.'

Mrs Hale could not speak, but she pressed her visitor's hand.

Mrs Thornton sighed. It was difficult to say that she would be kind to Margaret, whom she disliked so much. 'I am not the kind of person who shows affection, but I will be a true friend to Miss Hale. If she is in difficulty and comes to me for help, I will do everything I can for her. I also promise that if I ever see her doing something that I think is wrong, I will tell her, just as if she were my own daughter.'

There was a long pause. Mrs Hale felt that this promise did not include everything and she did not really understand why, but perhaps this was because she was very ill.

'I thank you,' she said. 'I shall never see you again in this world. But I thank you for your promise of kindness to my child.'

'Not kindness,' said Mrs Thornton, but fortunately Mrs Hale did not hear her.

Mrs Thornton held the dying woman's hand for a moment, and left the house without seeing anyone.

Meanwhile, Margaret and Dixon were discussing how to keep Frederick's visit a secret from anyone except the family. A letter was expected any day, and he would certainly arrive soon afterwards. They decided that if Dixon needed help in the kitchen they would ask Mary Higgins. They knew that if she met Frederick, who would be known as Mr Dickinson, she would not be interested in finding out more about him.

Poor Margaret! All that day she had to ignore her own feelings and look after her father, who sat in the sitting-room with his head in his arms. From time to time Mrs Hale suffered terrible pain, but in the evening she slept and Dixon sat with her. Darkness came. Margaret did not want to leave her father and the lamps had not been lit. She was sitting at the window looking out at the street when suddenly the doorbell rang.

She jumped up and went down to open the door. A tall man was standing there, but she could not see his face.

'Is this Mr Hale's?' he said clearly.

Margaret trembled all over, then whispered 'Frederick' and held out her arms to him. They kissed each other.

'Mother, is she alive?'

'She is very, very ill, but she is alive.'

'Thank God. Did you receive my letter?'

'No, but we knew you would come.'

Margaret took Frederick to Mr Hale's study and lit a lamp. Now she could see that his face was quite brown from the sun and that his eyes were very blue and bright. They did not exchange a word, but there was an immediate understanding between them and Margaret's heart was much lighter as she went upstairs.

It took Mr Hale some time to understand that Frederick had come, and when he did he began to cry like a child. Leaning on Margaret's arm, he went down to the study and Margaret left him with Frederick. She ran upstairs and cried bitterly; it was the first time she had allowed herself this relief for days. Frederick had come! He was safe! She could hardly believe it. Feeling much better, she went into the kitchen, made the fire, lit lamps and prepared food for the traveller.

She came into the study carrying the dishes like a servant, and Frederick immediately jumped up to take them from her; it was typical of his loving behaviour over the next few days. The brother and sister put some plates on the table, saying little, their hands touching, their eyes speaking to each other.

They heard Dixon moving about in the kitchen and Margaret went to tell her the news. Mrs Hale was awake but they decided that they would not tell her that Frederick had arrived until after Dr Donaldson's visit in the morning. He would be able to tell them how to prepare her for seeing her son.

Frederick and his father sat in the study talking while Margaret said nothing but listened quietly. It was a huge source of strength to her that her brother had come. She examined his appearance carefully and liked it. He had delicate features and a friendly, cheerful expression that could change suddenly and become very passionate. She could see that he understood his father's character and his weaknesses; he knew exactly how to talk to him and make him feel better. Perhaps because she was older now, the brother and sister felt closer to each other than ever before.

♦

When Mrs Hale saw Frederick the next morning, she seemed to improve. She sat with his hand in hers and would not let go of it even while she slept.

'I am very selfish,' she said, 'but it will not be for long.'

Frederick bent down and kissed the hand that imprisoned his.

Kind Dr Donaldson told Margaret that her mother did not have many hours to live, but Frederick could not believe it. That night, however, Mrs Hale became unconscious and died before morning. Frederick, who had been so strong until then, now sobbed so violently that Margaret and Dixon feared that their next-door-neighbours would hear him. Margaret sat with her father in her mother's room. He did not speak but from time to time stroked his wife's face, making a soft sound, like an animal with her young. He ignored Margaret completely and her heart ached for him so much that she could not think of her own loss at all.

Morning came and Margaret did her household duties, her eyes almost blinded with tears. Her father and brother were so full of grief that she felt she had to look after them. She made breakfast and lit a fire, but the contrast between its bright cheerfulness and her own thoughts made her kneel by the sofa and cry into the cushions. Dixon found her there and spoke gently to her, and the old servant's kindness made her feel a little better.

At breakfast Mr Hale did not seem to know where he was and Frederick burst into tears. Afterwards, when Margaret tried to discuss the arrangements for the funeral, Mr Hale understood almost nothing, but asked Margaret to write to his friend Mr Bell in Oxford and tell him the news.

Towards evening, Dixon told Margaret that she did not feel it was safe for Frederick to stay in Milton. She explained that while she was shopping she had met a young man called Leonards, whose family she had known in Southampton. He was a sailor and had been on the *Russell* at the same time as Frederick, although Dixon did not know if he had taken part in the mutiny. She had recognised Leonards and they had had a short conversation. He had asked about Frederick and talked about the mutiny, saying that Frederick would be hanged if he was caught. He said that a hundred pound reward had been offered for catching Frederick, and suggested that Dixon could help to trap him and that they would then share the reward. Dixon had never liked or trusted Leonards.

Her story made Margaret feel very uncomfortable. 'Have you told Frederick?' she asked.

'No, but I've told your father. And he thinks that Frederick must leave.'

The two women felt the same, but it was very hard for Margaret, just when Frederick had returned to his family. She was sitting by the fire and thinking about this, when Frederick came in.

'How tired you look, Margaret!' he said. 'You have been

looking after everybody and no one has looked after you. Lie on the sofa – there is nothing for you to do.'

Margaret gladly went to lie down and the two began to talk in low tones. Margaret told Frederick Dixon's story and he looked shocked.

'Leonards was the worst sailor on the ship – and a really nasty fellow! All the sailors who had the right ideas were angry with the captain, but Leonards was always trying to please him. And he's here, in Milton! If he knew I was here, he'd tell the police without a doubt.'

Mr Hale heard what they were saying and came towards them, eager and trembling. He took Frederick's hands in his.

'My boy, you must go. It is very bad – but you must. You have done all you could – you have been a comfort to your mother.'

'Perhaps I should stay and let them take me to court,' said Frederick thoughtfully.

'No, you must go.'

Frederick changed the subject. 'Do you know, I was in my bedroom this afternoon and the doorbell rang, so I waited for some time until I thought the visitor had left. Then I opened the door and saw a great, powerful fellow going down the stairs.'

'It was Mr Thornton,' said Mr Hale.

'Mr Thornton!' said Margaret, a little surprised. 'I thought you meant someone of a different class, not a gentleman.'

'He looked like someone who worked in a shop,' said Frederick carelessly, 'but it seems he is a manufacturer.'

Margaret was silent, remembering how, before she knew Mr Thornton well, she had thought of him in just the same way. She wanted to make Frederick understand what kind of person Mr Thornton was, but she could not think what to say.

Mr Hale continued, 'He came to offer to help us, but I could not see him. I told Dixon to ask if he wished to see you, Margaret.'

Margaret was silent and after some moments, Frederick said, 'It is painful to think I can never thank those who have shown you kindness. But you could both come to Spain. I have a good job there and a promise of promotion. Margaret, I told you about Dolores Barbour; she is not yet eighteen, but I hope that in a year she will be my wife. You would love her if you knew her, I am sure. If you came, you would have so many friends.'

'No – no more changes for me,' said Mr Hale. 'Moving here has cost me my wife. I am staying here.'

'Oh, Frederick, I am so glad you have someone to love and care for you out there,' said Margaret. 'I know you took part in the mutiny, but for Dolores' sake, perhaps you should try and prove that the most serious accusations are not true.'

A discussion began. Frederick did not know if it was possible to find the witnesses, all of them sailors, who could explain why the mutiny had happened.

'I don't think the attempt would be successful,' he said doubtfully.

'But could we not at least try to find them? There is a friend of mine – a lawyer, a very clever man – who would be happy to help you. Mr Henry Lennox, Father.' Margaret blushed when she said this.

'I think it is a good idea,' said Mr Hale, 'but Frederick must not stay in England just to see him.'

'Listen to my plan,' said Margaret. 'Frederick, you could take the night train to London tomorrow and leave a note from me for Mr Lennox at his home the following day. Then you could take the next boat from London.'

Mr Hale and Frederick immediately agreed to the plan and Frederick wrote down a list of sailors' names. Margaret wrote the note to Lennox with Frederick looking over her shoulder, and she did not have time to worry about whether she was using the right words after their last, difficult meeting.

♦

The family sat together in the sitting-room all the next day. Mr Hale only spoke when his children asked him questions. Frederick was now ashamed that he had allowed his grief to overcome him, and although his sorrow was very real, he did not speak about it again. Margaret was suffering more now and spent a lot of the time crying.

Mr Hale and Margaret wanted to make sure that Frederick was safely on the night train to London, and they decided that Margaret would accompany him to Outwood station. It was bitterly painful for Mr Hale to say goodbye to his son, and Margaret hurried Frederick into the carriage that was taking them there. They arrived at the station quite early and went to walk in a field next to the station. They were talking about their father when a horse rider passed slowly by. The evening sun was shining directly on Margaret's face and she bowed to the rider, who bowed stiffly back.

'Who is that?' asked Frederick.

'Mr Thornton – you saw him before, you know,' said Margaret, looking worried.

By now it was time to return to the station, and Frederick went to buy his ticket. They were walking down the railway platform when they heard the sound of the approaching train. Just then, a porter came up to them. It was clear that he was drunk, and he pushed Margaret to one side, then seized Frederick by his collar.

'Your name is Hale, I believe?'

When Frederick heard this, he immediately pushed the man away, and the porter fell off the platform, a distance of three or four feet.

'Run, run!' whispered Margaret urgently. 'The train is here. It was Leonards, wasn't it?'

A carriage door was open and Frederick jumped into the train. As he leaned out to say goodbye, the train started to leave and

Margaret was left standing alone. She felt so sick and faint that she went into the waiting room to sit down. When she felt a little better, she began to wonder if the man had been seriously hurt, and although she was frightened to do this, she went back to the platform to look for him. No one was there. She was trembling so much that she felt she could not walk home along the dark, lonely road, and she decided to take the next train back. But supposing Leonards recognised her as Frederick's companion?

Fortunately, when she went to get her ticket, there were only a few railway officials there, talking loudly to one another.

'So Leonards has been drinking,' said one of them. 'He came in about five minutes ago with a story about how he'd fallen off the platform. He wanted to borrow some money to go to London by the next train. I refused and he's gone off somewhere.'

'To have another drink, I'd guess,' said another man.

Frightened that Leonards would return, Margaret hid in the waiting room until the next train came. She was helped into the carriage by a porter whose face she did not dare to look at until the train started moving; then she saw that it was not Leonards.


## Chapter 10  A Police Inspector

Home seemed unnaturally calm after Margaret's frightening experience at the station. Mary Higgins had come to work in the kitchen. Mr Hale did nothing except sit in his chair in a kind of waking dream, and Margaret decided not to tell him about the incident at the station as things had ended well. Although it was possible that Leonards would borrow money to go to London, it was unlikely that he would find Frederick there. Margaret decided not to worry about something she could do nothing to prevent, as in a day or two Frederick would be safely out of England.

Mr Hale had wanted Mr Bell to come to the funeral, but his

old friend sent an affectionate letter saying that, unfortunately, he was unwell and could not come, although he promised to visit in September. Mr Hale decided to invite Mr Thornton instead, but Margaret, who feared the idea of seeing Mr Thornton again, begged her father not to ask him, and in the end he agreed.

♦

The morning of the funeral arrived. Margaret had slept badly and was shocked to receive a letter from Frederick saying that Mr Lennox was away and would not be back for another two days. Consequently, Frederick had decided to stay in London until his return. His decision made Margaret very anxious; if Leonards had gone to London, he now had more time to find Frederick. But she could not think about this for long; her father was almost too weak to get into the funeral carriage, and he needed all Margaret's attention and support.

When they arrived at the church for the funeral service, Margaret saw that Nicholas Higgins and Mary were there. She would have liked to talk to them but felt unable to leave her father. Mr Hale seemed to see nothing; he mechanically repeated the words of the clergyman, and at the end of the service he had to be led away as if he were blind.

Dixon covered her face with her handkerchief and was so absorbed in her grief that she did not notice that people were leaving until someone spoke to her. It was Mr Thornton. He had been standing at the back of the crowd with his head bent, and no one had recognised him.

'I'm sorry – but can you tell me how Mr Hale is? And Miss Hale too?'

'Of course, sir. Mr Hale is very distressed. Miss Hale seems better than you would expect.'

Mr Thornton would have preferred to hear that Margaret was really suffering. He was selfish enough to hope that his great love might be able to comfort her, but he was also disturbed by the memory of what he had seen at Outwood station. She had been with such a handsome young man and had seemed so relaxed and confident with him. What was she doing with a man at that late hour, so far away from home? All sorts of ideas went through his mind. Perhaps the reason why she was able to bear her grief was because of her love for this stranger!

Mr Thornton's face grew pale when he heard Dixon's answer and he said coldly, 'I suppose I may call – and see Mr Hale, I mean.'

He spoke as if he did not care at all, but although he hated Margaret at times, he desperately wanted to see her.

For some reason, Dixon never told Margaret about her meeting with Mr Thornton, and so Margaret never learnt that he had attended her poor mother's funeral.

◆

Although, to an observer, Margaret did not seem to feel much grief, her pain was in reality so great that sometimes she wanted to scream. What made her and her father feel even worse was that two days had passed and there was still no letter from Frederick. Mr Hale was walking up and down the sitting-room, desperate with worry, when Dixon opened the door to announce Mr Thornton. He took Mr Hale's hands and held them for a minute or two, his face and eyes showing more sympathy than could be put into words. Then he turned to Margaret.

She did not appear 'better than you would expect'. There was a look of great suffering on her face, and her eyes were red from crying. He had intended to greet her coldly, but he could not help going to her and speaking about her mother's death so gently that Margaret could not hide her emotion. She picked up her sewing and sat down. Mr Thornton's heart beat fast and for the moment he completely forgot about Outwood station.

Just then, Dixon came in and said, 'Miss Hale, there is someone to see you.'

She looked so upset that Margaret immediately thought that something had happened to Frederick. Feeling sick, she followed Dixon out of the room.

'It's a police inspector. He's in the study.'

'Did he name – ?'

'No. He just asked if he could speak to you.'

'Make sure Father does not come down.'

The inspector was a little surprised by Margaret's haughty manner as she entered the study. She showed neither surprise nor curiosity, but stood waiting for him to speak.

'I'm sorry, madam, but I need to ask you a few questions. A man called Leonards has died at the hospital. He had an accident – a fall – at Outwood station, between five and six last Thursday evening. The fall was not serious, but because of a previous illness and the man's alcohol habit, it killed him.'

Margaret's large eyes opened a little, but otherwise she showed no emotion at all. She said, 'Well – go on!'

'There will have to be an inquest,' said the inspector. He explained that a porter at the station had seen Leonards rudely push a young lady who was on the platform. She was with a companion who had then pushed Leonards off the edge of the platform. The porter said that he had not thought any more about the matter, because the platform was not high and he had seen Leonards get up and run down the platform.

'A grocer's assistant who was on the platform thinks that the woman may have been you, madam,' said the inspector, watching Margaret carefully.

'I was not there,' said Margaret expressionlessly.

The inspector bowed, but did not speak. The grocer's assistant had not been sure that it was her and he thought that she was probably telling the truth.

'Then, madam, you can assure me that you were not the companion of the gentlemen who pushed Leonards off the platform.'

'I was not there,' said Margaret slowly and heavily.

Margaret's exact repetition of her words made the inspector suspicious. Frowning, he said, 'I may have to call on you again this evening and ask you to appear at the inquest. You may need to give an alibi.'

When Margaret's haughty expression did not change, the inspector decided that the grocer's assistant was probably wrong.

'It is unlikely, madam, that this will happen. I hope you will forgive me for doing my duty.'

Margaret bowed her head as the inspector walked towards the door. She opened it for him and accompanied him to the front door. Then she returned to the study, locked the door and fainted.

♦

Mr Thornton and Mr Hale talked for some time. Margaret's father found Mr Thornton wonderfully kind and comforting, and trusted him enough to tell him his most secret feelings. At the end of their conversation both men felt much closer to each other. Mr Thornton left the house, and was walking along the street when he met the police inspector, who was called Watson. They knew one another and Mr Thornton had helped Watson get his first job.

They greeted each other in a friendly way and the police inspector said, 'I believe you were the magistrate who went to the hospital last night to hear the statement of a man called Leonards. He died several hours later.'

'Yes, I'm afraid he was a drunken fellow,' said Mr Thornton.

'Well, sir, his death is connected with somebody in the house I saw you coming out of just now – Mr Hale's house, I believe.'

'Yes,' said Mr Thornton, looking at the inspector with sudden interest. 'What about it?'

'There is some evidence that Miss Hale was the companion of the gentleman who pushed Leonards off the platform. A grocer's assistant who was there said that he recognised her, but the young lady denies that she was there at the time.'

'Miss Hale denies she was there?' said Mr Thornton.

'Yes, she denied it twice. Since you are the magistrate who saw Leonards, it seems a good idea to ask for your advice.'

'She denies having been at the station,' said Mr Thornton in a low tone. He paused and then said, 'You are quite right to ask for my advice. Don't do anything until you have seen me again. It's now three o'clock. Come to my factory at four.'

'I will, sir,' said Watson.

The two men separated and Mr Thornton hurried to the factory, went to his office and locked the door. There, he thought about every detail of his last two meetings with Margaret. She had looked so full of grief when he had seen her an hour ago that he had forgotten his suspicions. Now they were awakened again. Perhaps she was not as pure as she seemed; the thought came and then went immediately. But she had lied to the inspector, when she was usually so truthful. What did she fear would be revealed if she told the truth? Mr Thornton almost pitied her for the shame she must have felt to lie in this way.

Suddenly, he jumped up. As a magistrate, he could prevent the inquest; then Margaret would not have to give an alibi. Even if she was in love with another man, he could still save her from being shamed in public. He might despise her for lying, but he could still protect her.

He left his office and went out for about half an hour. When he returned, he wrote two lines on a piece of paper, which he put in an envelope. He instructed a clerk to give the note to Mr

Watson when he came at four o'clock. The note contained these words: 'There will be no inquest as the medical evidence shows that there is no reason for one. Do not investigate further. The decision is my responsibility.'

'Well,' thought Watson, 'that means I don't have to do a difficult job. None of my witnesses seemed certain of anything except the young woman.'

That evening, Watson visited the Hales' house again. Margaret had had a terrible day. She had decided to say nothing to either Dixon or her father about her meeting with the inspector, but lay on the sofa looking ill, only speaking when spoken to. She tried to smile when her father looked anxiously at her, but only succeeded in sighing. At nine o'clock the inspector had still not come and Mr Hale said goodnight and went to bed. Margaret was preparing to do the same when the doorbell rang. She answered the door herself and led the inspector into the study.

'You are late,' she said, hardly daring to breathe. 'Well?'

'I'm sorry to have given you unnecessary trouble, madam. They've decided not to have the inquest.'

'So there will be no more enquiries,' said Margaret.

'I believe I've got Mr Thornton's note with me,' said the inspector.

'Mr Thornton's!' said Margaret.

'Yes, he's a magistrate. Ah! Here it is.'

Margaret took it, but felt so confused that she could not understand what was written on the note. She held it in her hand and pretended to read it.

'I met Mr Thornton this morning, just as he was coming out of this house,' the inspector continued. 'He's an old friend of mine and he's also the magistrate who saw Leonards last night, so I explained my problem to him.'

Margaret sighed deeply. She was afraid of what she might hear and wished the man would go. She forced herself to speak.

'Thank you for calling. It is very late.'

He held out his hand for the note and she gave it back to him, then said, 'The writing is small and I could not read it. Could you read it to me?'

He read it aloud to her.

'You told Mr Thornton I was not there?'

'Oh, of course, madam. I'm sorry to have troubled you. The young man seemed so sure at first and now he says he was never sure at all. Good night, madam.'

She rang the bell and Dixon came to show the inspector out. As the servant returned up the passage, Margaret passed her.

'It is all right,' she said, without looking at her, and before Dixon could say anything, she ran upstairs to her bedroom and locked the door. Then she threw herself on her bed, feeling much too exhausted to do anything but lie motionless.

After half an hour, she felt a little better and sat up. Her first feeling was one of huge relief; there would be no inquest and so there was no danger that Frederick would be identified as her companion at the station. She then started to try and remember every word that the inspector had said about Mr Thornton. When had the inspector seen him? What had Mr Thornton said? What had he done? What were the exact words of his note? Until she could remember every word in the note, her mind refused to go further. But the facts were clear enough: Mr Thornton had seen her close to Outwood station last Thursday night and had been told that she had denied being there. Margaret did not tell herself that there was a good excuse for her lies. Nor did she imagine that Mr Thornton would be suspicious of the fact that she was with a handsome young man. There was only one thing that concerned her; the fact was that Mr Thornton now saw her as a liar. She was a liar and he knew it and must despise her for it.

'Oh, Frederick!' Margaret cried, 'What a price I have paid for saving you!'

She fell asleep with these thoughts going round and round in her mind.

When she woke the next morning, and the full memory of the situation returned to her, another thought came to her; it was because Mr Thornton had learnt about her denial that he had decided there would be no inquest. He had done this so that she would not have to give an alibi at the inquest. But if this were true, Margaret did not feel at all grateful, as it meant that he realised that she had done something very wrong. In that case, Margaret thought that he must feel great contempt for her. She hated the thought that he had saved her, and wondered what Leonards had told him. Perhaps he had told Mr Thornton about Frederick, or perhaps Mr Thornton had heard the story from Mr Bell. If so, then the mill owner had lied to save Mr Hale's son, who had come to see his dying mother. In that case, then she should be grateful to him. But she feared that he did not know the real facts and only saw her as a liar who must be saved. Margaret had always seen herself as superior to Mr Thornton. She was in a different position now and felt very unhappy about it. She did not ask herself why it mattered so much to her that Mr Thornton should despise her.

Dixon knocked at the door and came in. 'Here's something that will make you feel better – a letter from your brother.'

Margaret thanked Dixon, but waited until she was alone before she opened the letter. The first thing that she noticed was that the letter had been sent two days ago; it should have arrived the day before. Frederick wrote that he had seen Mr Lennox, who had said that it was very dangerous indeed for him to have returned to England. But after some discussion the lawyer had also agreed that it would be worthwhile finding witnesses who could tell the real story of what happened on the *Russell*. Then perhaps the trial could take place and the court would decide that Frederick was innocent.

'It seemed to me, little sister,' wrote Frederick, 'that your letter made him very anxious to help me. He's an intelligent fellow. I am on a boat that will leave in five minutes. What an escape that was! Don't tell anyone I came to England – not even the Shaws.'

Margaret could not have been more thankful that Frederick was safe. But the date on the letter told her that he had left England thirty hours ago! There had been no need for her to lie to the inspector and make Mr Thornton despise her! But why did she keep thinking about Mr Thornton? Why did she care so much about his opinion of her? What were these strong feelings that made her tremble and hide her face in the pillow?

She dressed and took the letter to her father, who she knew would not pay any attention to Frederick's words about the incident at the station. Mr Hale was very relieved that his son was safe but was concerned about Margaret, who seemed very distressed.

'Poor child, poor child,' he said and made her lie down on the sofa and cover herself with a shawl.

Through the day he tried hard to be cheerful, and Margaret was grateful to him. Mr Thornton had said that he might call that evening with a book for Mr Hale, but Margaret knew he would not come since he would be afraid of meeting her so soon after what had happened. She realised now that it was wrong of her to feel ungrateful. Oh, but she was grateful! It was a pleasure to her to realise how much she respected him.

The book from Mr Thornton arrived that evening with a kind note inside, but as Margaret had guessed, he did not come himself. By now, she felt very confused. She felt great shame when she thought about meeting him again, but at the same time she very much wanted to see him. But Mr Thornton did not come the next day, nor the day after that. This surprised and upset Mr Hale, as Mr Thornton had promised that he would call. Every time that the doorbell rang, both father and daughter hoped that it was the mill owner; but he did not come.

## Chapter 11  A Woman in Love

What most upset Mr Thornton about Margaret's lie was that it concerned an attractive young man. He could not forget that Margaret had looked at this man as if she loved him. And then there was the fact that she had been with him in the evening, when it was growing dark, at some distance from home. The fact that she had lied showed that she had done something wrong and needed to hide it. Mr Thornton decided that Margaret, who was usually so truthful, was prepared to do something wrong because of her love for this stranger. This thought made him fiercely jealous and very bad-tempered. At home he was more than usually silent, and annoyed his mother by walking up and down the sitting-room without speaking.

'Can you stop – can you sit down for a moment?' said his mother crossly one evening. 'I have something to tell you.'

He sat down and Mrs Thornton continued, 'Betsy is so upset by her lover's death that she cannot work for us any more and is going to leave us.'

'Her lover was Leonards, you told me.'

'Yes. And she has told me that Miss Hale was with the young man who pushed Leonards off the platform. She was walking in a field with him, apparently, quite late in the evening.'

'I don't see why that should concern us.'

'I am glad to hear you say so,' said Mrs Thornton, looking pleased. 'But I – I made a promise to her mother that if her daughter did something wrong, I would speak to her about it.'

'I don't see any harm in what she did that evening,' said Mr Thornton, getting up and turning his face away.

'You would not have approved if Fanny had done it.'

'Miss Hale and Fanny are very different. Miss Hale always has a good reason for doing something, unlike Fanny.'

'How kind you are about your sister! Miss Hale's behaviour is clear to me now. The man she was with is her lover.'

Mr Thornton turned round to look at his mother, his face very grey and said, 'Yes, mother, I do believe he is her lover.'

The pain of admitting this was almost too much to bear, and he turned away from her, then immediately turned round again and said, 'Mother, he is her lover. But she may need help and advice. I know that something is wrong – she is in difficulty. Go to her and advise her.'

'What do you mean, John?' said his mother, really shocked. 'What do you know?'

He did not answer, and after some moments she said, 'I will go to her and speak to her as if she were Fanny and had gone walking with a young man in the evening. Then I shall have kept my promise to her mother and done my duty.'

'You cannot talk to her in that way. She is much too proud.'

'I can and I will.'

'Well,' Mr Thornton said, going to the door, 'don't tell me any more about it. I can't bear to think about it.'

'Oh, Margaret, could you not have loved me?' he said fiercely to himself, as he locked himself in his office. 'I may not be a gentleman, but I would never have made you lie for me.'

♦

Margaret was sitting alone, writing a letter to Edith, when Dixon opened the door to announce Mrs Thornton. Margaret was so gentle and polite that Mrs Thornton found it very difficult to say her carefully prepared words. It was only as she stood up to leave that she coughed and said, 'Miss Hale, I promised your mother that if you behaved badly in any way, I would do my

70

duty and give you my opinion of your behaviour.'

Margaret blushed. She thought that Mrs Thornton was going to speak to her about the lie she had told, and that Mr Thornton had asked her to do this.

Mrs Thornton continued, 'At first, when I heard that you had been seen walking with a gentleman, in the evening, as far away from home as Outwood station, I could hardly believe it. But my son confirmed the story. It was not at all wise of you, Miss Hale. The story could harm your reputation.'

Margaret's eyes flashed fire. So Mrs Thornton had not come to talk to her about the fact that she had lied. Instead, Mrs Thornton wanted to discuss her behaviour, when she hardly knew her at all! It was too rude!

Seeing how angry Margaret was, Mrs Thornton became angry too. 'For your mother's sake, I felt it was my duty to talk to you about your behaviour.'

'For my mother's sake!' exclaimed Margaret tearfully. 'She never wished you to insult me, I am sure.'

'Insult you, Miss Hale!'

'Yes, madam,' said Margaret more steadily. 'What do you know about me that would make you suspect – Oh!' she said, covering her face with her hands, 'I know now, Mr Thornton has told you – '

'No, Miss Hale,' said Mrs Thornton, 'Mr Thornton has told me nothing. Listen, young lady, and you will understand what kind of man you have refused. This Milton manufacturer, whom you despise so much, told me that he believed that you were in difficulties because of a gentleman and that you needed some advice. He admitted that you had been seen with a gentleman at Outwood station; but apart from that, he has said nothing.'

Margaret was still crying, with her face hidden in her hands, and Mrs Thornton softened and said, 'Perhaps there are circumstances that can explain your behaviour.'

Margaret considered what to say but could not find a good explanation. Finally, she said in a low voice, 'I can give you no explanation. I have done wrong, but not in the way you think. I think Mr Thornton judges me more kindly than you.'

'It is the last time I shall try to give you advice,' said Mrs Thornton stiffly. 'I only came because your mother asked me to. I never liked the fact that my son cared for you. You did not appear to be good enough for him. But your behaviour during the riot showed that you cared for him too. When the servants and workers started talking about you, I felt that it was right for him to ask you to marry him. But when he came to see you, your feelings had changed. I told him that I thought that perhaps your lover – '

'What must you think of me, madam?' said Margaret, throwing back her head haughtily. 'Please do not continue. I will not try to explain my actions. You must allow me to leave.' And she left the room with the noiseless grace of a princess.

Mrs Thornton was not particularly annoyed by Margaret's behaviour; she did not care enough about her for that. The fact that her words had upset Margaret pleased her, as it showed that Margaret cared about what people thought of her. 'I like to see a girl get angry at the idea of being talked about,' thought Mrs Thornton. 'It shows that she has the right kind of pride.'

♦

After she had left Mrs Thornton, Margaret went to her room and made herself recall every word they had spoken. Then she said sadly to herself, 'Her words can't really affect me because I was not with a lover, I was with Frederick! But it's awful, knowing that she thinks this about me. She doesn't know my real sin – that I lied. He never told her – I should have known he would not!'

Then a new thought came to her. 'He too must think poor

Frederick is my lover. I understand now. It's bad enough that he knows that I lied, but he also believes that someone else cares for me, and that I – Oh dear! Why do I care about what he thinks? I don't know why, but I am very miserable. He misunderstands me so completely and I feel terrible!'

She jumped up. 'No, I will not examine my own feelings. It would be useless. If I live to be an old woman, perhaps I'll sit by the fire and think about the life I might have had. There must be many women who have made the same mistake and only realise when it's too late. I was so rude to him that day! But I did not understand my feelings then. I don't even know when they began. I must be strong. It will be difficult, but when I see him I will be very calm and quiet. But I may not see him; he has not called for some days. That would be worst of all.'

To try and forget about her feelings, Margaret decided to visit the Higgins' next-door-neighbours, the Bouchers, but when she arrived at their house, a neighbour told her that Mrs Boucher was dying. A doctor had been called and the children were being looked after by neighbours. Margaret decided that the best thing she could do was call on the Higgins. She went next door and found Nicholas Higgins playing with the three youngest Boucher children.

'Have you seen Mr Thornton?' she asked Nicholas.

'Yes,' said Nicholas angrily.

'He refused you?' said Margaret sorrowfully.

'Of course he did. I knew he would.'

'I am sorry I asked you. You told him I sent you?

'I don't know if I mentioned your name. I said a woman had advised me to ask him.'

'I am disappointed in Mr Thornton,' said Margaret.

There was a slight noise behind her. Margaret turned round and saw Mr Thornton standing at the door with a look of angry surprise on his face. In one quick movement, Margaret stood up and left without saying a word. As she hurried to Mrs Boucher's, she heard the door shut loudly behind her.

Mr Thornton had come to see Higgins because, although he tried to hide it, there was a part of him that was very soft. He had refused Higgins because he had heard reports that the man was a troublemaker, but afterwards he had learnt that Higgins had waited five hours to see him and he was impressed by the man's patience; he had also learnt that the worker's story about the Boucher family was true. He had come to Higgins's house to offer him work.

Higgins was a proud man; there was a long pause before he accepted the offer, but he did and the two men shook hands.

'Was that the woman who advised you to ask me for work?' asked Mr Thornton.

Higgins told him that it was. Mr Thornton frowned, disliking the idea that Margaret might think he had given Higgins work because of her, when he was only doing what was right.

As Mr Thornton left, Margaret came out of the Bouchers' house. She did not see him, and he followed her, admiring her tall, graceful figure. Then he suddenly felt very jealous. He wanted to speak to her and see how she would behave after all that had happened. Also, he had heard her last words and wanted her to know that he had given Higgins work.

He came up to her and she looked at him in surprise.

'You do not need to be disappointed in me, Miss Hale. I have given Higgins work.'

'I am glad,' said Margaret coldly.

There was a silence and then Mr Thornton said, 'Miss Hale, have you no explanation for the lie that you told? You must know what it has made me think.'

Margaret said nothing. She was wondering whether she could give some kind of an explanation and still be loyal to Frederick.

'No,' said Mr Thornton, 'I will ask no more questions. Believe me, your secret is safe with me. But please be careful. I am now only speaking as a friend of your father.'

'I am aware of that,' said Margaret, forcing herself to appear uninterested. 'But the secret is about another person, and I cannot explain it without harming him.'

'I have no desire to know the gentleman's secrets,' said Mr Thornton angrily. 'My only interest in you is – as a friend. That is all, now. You believe me, Miss Hale?'

'Yes,' said Margaret quietly and sadly.

'Then really, I don't see why we should continue walking together. I thought perhaps that you might have something to say, but I see that we mean nothing to each other. If you are quite certain that I no longer have any strong feelings for you, then I wish you good afternoon.' And he walked away.

'What can he mean?' wondered Margaret. 'He talks as if I thought he still cared about me, when I know he cannot. His mother will have said all those cruel things about me. But I will try my best not to care about him. Surely I can control this wild, miserable feeling that tempted me to betray Frederick, just so that he would respect me again. I must be strong – I must!'

♦

Several months passed, and although Mr Thornton occasionally came for lessons with Mr Hale, he never asked to see Margaret. After her conversation in the street with Mr Thornton, Margaret's moods varied strangely, but a letter from Edith made her feel a little less miserable, as her cousin talked about returning to Harley Street in about six months and inviting her to stay. Life became quiet and boring. Margaret looked after the house and her father, visited Mary Higgins and helped to care for the Boucher children after the death of their mother. Then in September, as he had promised, Mr Bell came to visit. Mr Hale's old friend liked Margaret enormously and they immediately became very good friends.

'I must say, I think your opinions are very old-fashioned,' said Margaret jokingly to Mr Bell one afternoon.

'Listen to this daughter of yours, Hale. What has life in Milton done to her? She has become a democrat!'

'You say that just because I believe that commerce is good for the country.'

'I don't like this rushing around, with everybody trying to get rich. I don't believe there's a man in Milton who knows how to sit still. That reminds me, Mr Thornton is coming to tea tonight,' said Mr Bell, not noticing that Margaret became very quiet.

Mr Thornton was still in love with Margaret, despite all his efforts not to be. He had tried hard not to see her, but in his dreams she came dancing towards him with open arms. He came late to the Hales' house and, to avoid meeting her, spent a long time talking about business matters with Mr Bell. He was bad-tempered and cross and Mr Bell thought he had become quite a rude fellow. At last they went upstairs and found Margaret holding a letter, which she was eagerly discussing with her father.

'It is a letter from Henry Lennox,' said Mr Hale to Mr Bell. 'It makes Margaret very hopeful.'

Mr Bell nodded. Mr Thornton looked at Margaret, who blushed, and he wanted to leave and never return again.

A conversation began about the differences between Oxford University, where Mr Bell taught, and Milton, where he had lived as a child. Mr Bell talked about the importance of tradition, history and learning, while Mr Thornton felt that action and living in the present mattered more. Mr Bell joked a lot, and Margaret saw that this upset Mr Thornton, who wanted a serious conversation.

Trying to change the subject, she said, 'Edith says that cotton materials in Corfu are cheaper and better than those in London.'

'Are you sure?' said her father. 'I think Edith is exaggerating.'

'If Margaret is sure, then I am too,' said Mr Bell. 'Margaret, you are such a truthful person, I don't believe that anyone who is a relation of yours could exaggerate.'

'Is Miss Hale so well-known for truthfulness?' said Mr Thornton, bitterly. The moment he said this, he could have bitten his tongue out. Why was he so evil tonight and why was he so cross with Mr Bell, his kind old friend?

Margaret did not get up and leave as she would have done formerly. She glanced at Mr Thornton in sad surprise, with the expression of a hurt child, then bent over her sewing and did not speak again.

Mr Thornton could not help looking at her and he saw that when she sighed, her whole body trembled. He desperately wanted her to look at him and speak to him, so that he could show her he was sorry, but she did not raise her head. She could not care for him, he thought. He gave short, sharp answers to the older men's questions and left rather suddenly. As he walked home, he thought that he was right to see Margaret as little as possible; her power over him was too great.

When the mill owner left, Margaret silently began to fold up her work, looking completely exhausted. As the three prepared for bed, Mr Bell said, 'Success has spoiled that man. He used to be a simple, honest fellow. Now, everything offends him.'

'He was not his usual self tonight,' Margaret said quickly. 'Something must have happened to upset him.'

Mr Bell looked at her sharply. After she had left the room, he said, 'Hale, have you ever thought that Thornton and your daughter might be fond of each other?'

'Never!' said Mr Hale, astonished by the idea. 'I am sure you are wrong. If there is anything, it is all on Mr Thornton's side.'

'I would say that she showed quite a few signs tonight!'

'I am sure you are wrong,' said Mr Hale. 'Margaret has been almost rude to Mr Thornton at times.'

'Well, it was only a suggestion. And whether I'm right or wrong, I'm very sleepy.'

Mr Bell left the next day, telling Margaret that she must come to him if she was in difficulty. To Mr Hale he said, 'That Margaret of yours has gone deep into my heart. Take care of her – she is a very precious creature. I wish you'd leave Milton, Hale! It is completely unsuitable for you, and I'm sorry I recommended it. You and Margaret could come and live with me. I would like that very much. What do you think?'

'Never!' said Mr Hale. 'My one great change has been made, and it has caused me great suffering. I will live here and I will be buried here.'

'Well, we will forget it for the moment. Margaret, give me a goodbye kiss. Remember, I am always here for you.'


## Chapter 12  Mr Hale

After Mr Bell's departure, life returned to what it had been before his visit. Four months passed. Margaret tried to keep herself busy visiting the Boucher children, and was always kind and attentive to her father, but the truth was that she felt bored and miserable. Mr Thornton seldom came to his lessons, partly because, as a result of the strike, his business affairs had become more complicated. When he did come, he never asked to see Margaret, and often sent a note at the last moment, saying that he was too busy for a lesson. Although Mr Hale had new pupils to replace Mr Thornton, he missed their conversations and became quite depressed by his pupil's frequent absences.

One February evening Mr Hale, blushing as he asked the question, suddenly said, 'Margaret, have you ever had any reason to think that Mr Thornton cared for you?'

Margaret did not answer immediately, then bent her head and said, 'Yes. I believe – oh, Father, I should have told you.' And dropping her work, she hid her face in her hands.

'No dear, there was no need. I am sure you would have told me if you had returned his feelings. Did he speak to you about it?'

No answer at first, then a slow 'Yes'.

'And you refused him?'

A long sigh and another 'Yes'. Then, blushing even more, she said, 'Now, Father, I have told you this, but I cannot tell you more – it is too painful for me. Oh, Father, it is because of me that Mr Thornton is no longer your friend, and I am so sorry; but I could not help it.'

They were quiet for some minutes. Mr Hale stroked Margaret's cheek and was almost shocked to find her face wet with tears. As he touched her, she jumped up, smiling brightly, and began to talk about the Lennoxes with such eagerness to change the subject that he was too kind to refer to it again.

'Tomorrow – yes, tomorrow the Lennoxes will be back in Harley Street. How strange it will be! Imagine, Edith a mother!'

'Why don't you go and see them for a fortnight?' said her father. 'It would be very good for you, and Mr Lennox could tell you his latest news about Frederick.'

'No, Father, you need me here,' said Margaret. After a pause, she continued sadly, 'I am losing hope about Frederick. Mr Lennox is trying to tell us the news gently, but you can see from his letters that he thinks there is no hope of finding witnesses.'

A few days later, Margaret's feelings were confirmed when Frederick wrote saying that he had received a letter from Henry

Lennox stating that it was unlikely that the witnesses could be found. Frederick angrily said that he no longer considered himself English, which made Margaret cry. But in March, a much happier letter arrived; Frederick and Dolores had got married. Dolores's family owned a large manufacturing company and Frederick was now certain to achieve a high position in it. Margaret smiled a little when she learnt this, remembering her former dislike of trade. And now her brother was a trader! Well, it did not matter at all, and Frederick was very, very happy.

♦

Spring came, and Margaret became a little worried about her father, who occasionally had difficulty breathing. When Mr Bell invited them to visit him in Oxford, she persuaded Mr Hale to accept, hoping that it would improve his health. The invitation included Margaret, but she decided to stay at home; with her father away, she would have no responsibilities and would be able to rest, something that she had not been able to do since she came to Milton.

Margaret was astonished at how relieved she felt once her father had left. The pressure was gone; there was no-one who depended on her for comfort and entertainment. For months, she had had no time to think about her problems, but now she could examine them one by one and give each of them the right place in her life. She sat almost motionless for hours, remembering every detail of her relationship with Mr Thornton.

After two days of silent thinking, she decided that if only she could be friends with him again, or even if he would visit her father more often, she would feel happier. But when she went to bed that night, a feeling of sorrow and anxiety still remained.

That April evening, Margaret had found that she could not stop thinking about her father. Strangely, that same night, in Oxford, all Mr Hale's thoughts were about his daughter. His old friends there were very kind to him, but the unfamiliar social activity had made him feel quite exhausted.

'I am tired,' he told Mr Bell. 'But I am fifty-five years old.'

'Nonsense! I'm over sixty. You're quite a young man.'

Mr Hale shook his head. 'These last few years –' he said. And then, after a pause, he went on, 'About Margaret. If I die – '

'Nonsense!'

'I often think – what will happen to her? I suppose the Lennoxes will ask her to live with them. I hope they will.'

'You know how fond I am of that girl, Hale. She has made me her slave! I will look after her, and when I die, everything I have will be hers. But you're a thin, healthy fellow, unlike me. There are no prizes for guessing who will die first.'

But Mr Bell was wrong, and that night Mr Hale lay down in his bed for the last time. The servant who entered in the morning received no answer to his words. Mr Hale's heart had stopped during the night, but his calm, beautiful face showed no pain, only the white, cold look of death.

Mr Bell was so shocked that he could not speak for some time. Then he told his servant to pack his bags, and took the next train to Milton. There was only one person sitting near him. The man's face was hidden behind a newspaper and it was some time before Mr Bell realised that it was Mr Thornton.

The two shook hands, and when Mr Bell told the mill owner the bad news, Mr Thornton said nothing for over a quarter of an hour. Finally he said, 'What about –?' and stopped suddenly.

'Margaret, you mean. Yes, I am going to Milton to tell her. I will look after her as if she were my own child. I would like her to come and live me, but there are those Lennoxes!'

'Who are they?' asked Mr Thornton, trembling with interest.

'Oh, fashionable London people. Captain Lennox married her cousin – the girl she was brought up with. And there's her aunt, Mrs Shaw. And then there's that brother.'

'What brother?'

'The brother of Captain Lennox – a clever young lawyer. I'm told he's been interested in Margaret for a long time. Now that she will have money, he will be even more interested in her.'

'What money?' asked Mr Thornton, far too interested to realise how rude the question was.

'Well, she'll have my money at my death.'

Mr Thornton became very silent when he heard this. Finally, Mr Bell asked him where he had been and the mill owner explained that he had been to France on business.

'Ah, commerce! Poor old Hale! Milton is so different from Helstone – a charming little village in the New Forest.'

'I understand it was a great change for Mr Hale.'

When Mr Bell arrived at the house in Compton, Margaret, who was standing at an upstairs window, saw him get out of the carriage alone and guessed the truth immediately. She stood in the middle of the sitting room, looking as if she had been turned into stone.

'Oh, don't tell me! I know it from your face! You would not have left him – if he were alive! Oh, Father, Father!'

◆

The shock was very great, and for more than two days Margaret lay on the sitting-room sofa with her eyes closed, hardly speaking at all. Mr Bell needed to return to Oxford and make arrangements for the funeral, which would be held there rather than in Milton, because of the problems of transporting the body. However, it was clear that Margaret was not well enough to travel to Oxford to attend the funeral. After a lot of thought, Mr Bell decided to write to Mrs Shaw, who had returned to England, and ask her to come to Milton. His letter to her had an immediate effect, and the following day she travelled up by train.

Margaret was the first to hear her aunt's carriage when it

stopped in front of the house. Her whole face trembled, and when Mr Bell came up with Mrs Shaw, she was standing up, looking very unsteady. Her aunt opened her arms and Margaret went into them and started to cry.

Mr Bell crept out of the room and went down to the study. There, he tried to forget his troubles by examining the books, but they only reminded him of his dead friend. He was glad to hear the sound of Mr Thornton's voice at the front door and called out, 'Thornton, is that you? Come in for a minute or two.'

The mill owner joined him and Mr Bell told him that Mrs Shaw had come to look after Margaret.

'The woman has brought a servant with her, and I shall have to leave and find somewhere to stay.'

'Come and stay with us. We have five or six empty bedrooms.'

'Then I'll just go upstairs and say goodbye to the poor girl and that aunt, and leave with you immediately.'

It was some time before Mr Bell came down again, and as they set out for Marlborough Street he explained why.

'Mrs Shaw is anxious to return home with Margaret as soon as possible. She doesn't seem to understand that the girl cannot travel in her present condition. Margaret said she has friends she must see, but then she started crying and said she was glad to leave a place where she had suffered so much. I must return to Oxford tomorrow, so a decision must be made.'

Mr Thornton did not reply. The words 'She was glad to leave a place where she had suffered so much' were going round and round in his head. So that was the way Margaret would remember her time in Milton, when to him every moment he had spent with her had been so precious.

They arrived in Marlborough Street and Mrs Thornton, after welcoming Mr Bell, asked how Margaret was.

'She seems completely broken. I would like her to live with me but she has relations who want her to live with them in London.'

'Where have these relations been, when Miss Hale has had so many troubles?'

Having asked the question, Mrs Thornton, who felt no interest in the answer, left to prepare Mr Bell's room.

'They have been living abroad,' Mr Bell said. 'The aunt brought her up, and Margaret and her cousin have been like sisters. But I wanted her as a child of my own, and I am jealous of these people who don't seem to have looked after her properly. It would be different if Frederick claimed her.'

'Frederick!' exclaimed Mr Thornton. 'Who is he?'

'Frederick!' said Mr Bell in surprise. 'Don't you know? He's her brother. Have you not heard – ?'

'I have never heard his name before. Where is he? Who is he?'

'He is the son who was involved in that mutiny.'

'I had never heard of him until this moment. Where does he live?'

'In Spain. He's likely to be arrested if he comes to England.'

'Was he here in Milton at the time of Mrs Hale's death?'

'No, it's not possible. What made you think he was?'

'I saw a young man walking with Miss Hale one day,' replied Mr Thornton, 'and I think it was about that time.'

'Oh, that was probably young Lennox, the Captain's brother. He's a lawyer and Margaret and he write to each other. Do you know,' said Mr Bell, watching Mr Thornton carefully, 'when I last came here I wondered if you perhaps cared for Margaret.'

'I admired Miss Hale, as everyone must. She is a beautiful creature,' said Mr Thornton quickly.

'Is that all? A beautiful creature! You talk about her as if she were a horse or dog!'

Mr Thornton's eyes flashed for a moment. 'Mr Bell,' he said, 'you should remember that not every man can talk about their feelings as freely as you. Let us talk about something else.'

The two men began to discuss business matters. A new building was being put up in Mr Thornton's factory yard and Mr Bell asked what it would be. Mr Thornton explained that he planned it as a dining-room for his workers and told Mr Bell the following story. He had slowly become friendly with one of his workers, a man called Higgins. Passing by the man's house one day, he had called on him, and had been shocked to see how little the family had to eat, and what bad quality the meat was. After discussions with Higgins, the mill owner decided to buy large quantities of good-quality food at a cheap price, and to provide a large oven at the mill and a cook. For some months now, the workers had been able to have a good lunch there. Mr Thornton had even started eating with the men from time to time and was enjoying his conversations with them.

'I am really getting to know some of them now. They have such a sense of humour! But it is not a charity and the men pay me rent for the oven and the cooking-place at the back of the mill. They will have to pay more for the dining-room.'

♦

Mrs Shaw hated noisy, smoky Milton and wanted to return to London the day after the funeral in Oxford. Margaret was too weak and exhausted to resist her and it was agreed that she would return with her aunt, and that Dixon would stay behind to pack up the furniture.

The day before the funeral Margaret received a letter from Mr Bell in Oxford:

'My dear Margaret,
    I intended to return to Milton after the funeral but

unfortunately I have duties here that mean I cannot come. Captain Lennox and Mr Thornton are here. The Captain will come to Milton to take you and his mother home and I have asked my lawyer to arrange the sale of your house. Now, there is something else. You may not know this, but I told your father that when I die you will inherit my money and my possessions. I don't intend to die yet, of course! But meanwhile, I would like to make a formal arrangement to give you £250 a year. It is yours and you can pay the Lennoxes this for as long as you live with them. They can then pay for Dixon. I will make another arrangement about money for your needs – items such as pretty dresses and chocolate! Now, Margaret, you may be wondering what right an old man has to settle your affairs in this way. But I have loved your father for thirty-five years, and I have no relations to look after or give my money to. Please make an old man happy and tell me that Margaret Hale is not the girl to say no. Write to me, and tell me your answer. But *do not thank me.*'

After reading this, Margaret took a pen and wrote with a trembling hand, 'Margaret Hale is not the girl to say no.'

For the next two days, she wandered round the house, trying to decide which things she wanted to keep. She asked Dixon to take one of her father's books to Mr Thornton after she had left, and wrote a note to him very quickly.

The day after the funeral, she took a carriage to the Higgins' and said a sad goodbye to them. Feeling that she should also say goodbye to Mrs Thornton, although she did not wish to do this, she went to visit her with her aunt, and Mrs Thornton, looking kinder than ever before, was introduced to Mrs Shaw.

'Where are you going to live, Miss Hale?' Mrs Thornton asked. 'Mr Bell told me that you were going to leave Milton.'

'My niece will live with me in London. She is almost like a daughter to me,' said her aunt, looking fondly at Margaret.

At this moment, Mr Thornton entered the room; he had only just returned from Oxford.

'John,' said his mother, 'this lady is Mrs Shaw, Miss Hale's aunt. I am sorry to say that Miss Hale's visit is to say goodbye.'

'You are going then?' he said in a low voice.

'Yes,' said Margaret. 'We leave tomorrow.'

Mr Thornton turned away and seemed to be examining something on the table. He did not even seem to be aware that they had got up to leave, but he went outside with them and helped Mrs Shaw into the carriage.

He and Margaret were standing close together on the doorstep, and the memory of the day of the riot came back to both of them. He thought of how cruel she had been to him when he had gone to see her the next day, and although his heart was beating fast with his love for her, he told himself, 'Let her go, with her stony heart and her beauty. How coldly she looks at me! Let her go!'

And there was no tone of regret or emotion in his voice as he said goodbye. He took the hand she offered to him as if it were a dead flower; but no one saw Mr Thornton again that day.


## Chapter 13   A New Life

Edith gave birth to her second child and, as was the custom, remained quietly in her room for several weeks afterwards. Consequently, the house in Harley Street was less busy than usual, and Margaret was able to rest and try to understand the sudden change that had taken place in her life. Once again, she was well looked after and living in a luxurious house. Mrs Shaw and Edith were delighted that she had returned 'home', and Captain Lennox was kind and brotherly to her. Margaret felt that it was almost ungrateful of her to have a secret feeling that the Helstone vicarage and even the little house in Milton were much more like her idea of 'home'.

Just as she was starting to feel bored, Edith came downstairs and the normal life of the household began again. As she used to do, Margaret answered her cousin's notes for her and reminded her of her social engagements. She loved playing with Sholto, Edith's little boy, and looked after both children while the servants had lunch. But because her father had died so recently, she was not yet able to go out socially, and while the rest of the family went out almost every day, she was often left alone. Then her thoughts returned to Milton and she compared her life there with her comfortable life in Harley Street. She was becoming bored and was afraid that she would forget that there was a world of servants and workers, with all their hopes and fears. There seemed to be an emptiness in her life now. When she suggested this to Edith, her cousin stroked her cheek and said, 'Poor child! Soon, when Henry returns from his travels, we will start having dinner parties again, and you will feel more cheerful, poor darling!' But Margaret did not feel that dinner parties were the answer to her problems.

Dixon was still in Milton and Margaret missed her greatly. She read the servant's letters eagerly, hoping for news of friends. Dixon mentioned Mr Thornton quite frequently, as he often gave her advice about the Hales' business affairs. Then, at the end of June, when the house in Milton had been sold, she came to London in her new role as Margaret's servant. She brought a lot of Milton gossip with her. Fanny Thornton had got married and had had a very grand wedding, paid for by her brother. Dixon had organised a sale of furniture, and Mrs Thornton had bought several pieces and paid too little, while Mr Thornton had bought others and paid too much. She did not have much to say about the Higgins family but believed that Nicholas was well. She had heard that Mary had gone to work at Mr Thornton's

88

mill as a cook, which sounded strange to her – why did the mill need a cook?

Henry Lennox, who had been doing legal work in another part of the country, returned to London and, as he had done in the past, spent a lot of time in Harley Street. He seemed even cleverer than before, although Margaret thought he had become colder. But the two shared similar intellectual interests, and unlike Edith and the Captain, they enjoyed discussing a variety of subjects. Indeed, Margaret suspected that Mr Lennox felt slightly contemptuous of his brother and sister-in-law and their aimless way of life. He and Margaret often saw each other, but always in the presence of others, and this helped them to relax and forget their embarrassment. Margaret suspected that Mr Lennox tried to avoid being alone with her. But when he had made a particularly clever remark, she noticed that he would glance at her as if he wanted to know what she thought of it.

♦

Mr Bell wrote frequently, and in August Margaret received a letter from him saying that he would visit her the following week. For several months he had been complaining that he felt unwell, and some days before his visit, he wrote to say that he would come on Wednesday instead of Monday. But on Wednesday he did not appear, and the next morning a letter arrived from his servant explaining that Mr Bell had postponed his visit because he had suddenly felt ill. Then, at the time that he was supposed to leave for London, he had suffered a heart attack, and the doctors did not think he would survive the night.

Margaret received this letter at breakfast time and her face went very pale as she read it; she silently put the letter into Edith's hands and left the room. Her cousin was very shocked by the news and started to cry, but when she had recovered a little, she went upstairs and found Dixon packing a small case.

Margaret, who was putting on her hat, was sobbing, her hands trembling so much that she could hardly tie the strings.

It was quickly agreed that Captain Lennox would accompany her to Oxford, and before midday the two were sitting in a train carriage. They arrived at Mr Bell's house and learned that he had died during the night. The news could not have been worse, but Margaret was glad that she was able to see the room where her father had died, and that she could say a quiet goodbye to the cheerful old man who had loved her so much.

Captain Lennox fell asleep on the journey home and Margaret spent the time crying and thinking of how, in the last year, she had lost her mother, her father, and now Mr Bell. It seemed too much to bear, but then she arrived in Harley Street and Edith and her aunt were so kind and gentle, and little Sholto was so happy to see her, that she began to feel better. And by the time she went up to bed, she was able to thank God that her dear old friend had suffered so little.

'Will Margaret inherit Mr Bell's money?' whispered Edith to her husband when she was alone with him that night.

The Captain, however, had no idea, and did not think that Mr Bell had much money at all. Edith was disappointed to hear this, but a week later she came dancing towards her husband and said, 'I am right and you are wrong, sir. Margaret has had a lawyer's letter and she will inherit about £2,000 pounds, and also Mr Bell's property in Milton, which is worth about £40,000.'

'She will be a rich woman! And what does she say about it?'

'Oh, she has known about it for some months, apparently, but had no idea it was so much. She says she is afraid of the money. But that's nonsense and she'll soon get used to it.'

It seemed natural that Henry Lennox would be Margaret's legal adviser, and he often came to her with papers that needed signing.

'Henry,' said Edith one day, with a little smile, 'do you know how I expect your long conversations with Margaret to end?'

'No, I don't,' he said, reddening. 'And I don't wish you to tell me. What you are thinking of may or may not happen. Please don't say anything to Margaret. She has been quite cool to me for a long time and is only just beginning to be kind.'

♦

Autumn came and the family went on holiday to Cromer, a pretty town on the east coast. Margaret's troubles had made her quite weak, and the fresh sea air was just what she needed. She spent long hours sitting on the beach, and the gentle sound of the waves, and the beauty of the sea and sky, calmed her spirit. While Aunt Shaw went shopping and Edith and Captain Lennox went horse-riding, Margaret thought about her time in Milton. Her greatest regret was that Mr Thornton had never learnt the truth about why she had lied. But slowly she began to realise that she had a future, and her face, which had looked so pale and tight with pain, began to change.

After three weeks Henry Lennox, who had been in Scotland on business, came to join them, and he immediately noticed the difference in Margaret.

'The sea has done Miss Hale a lot of good,' he said one afternoon, when she had left the room. 'She looks ten years younger than she did in Harley Street.'

'It's the hat I got her,' said Edith delightedly. 'I knew it would suit her the moment I saw it.'

'I'm sorry,' said Mr Lennox, 'but I believe I know the difference between a pretty dress and a pretty woman. No hat could make Miss Hale's eyes so bright or her lips so red. Her face is full of peace and light. She is even more beautiful than ...' he lowered his voice, 'the Margaret Hale of Helstone.'

From this time, the clever and ambitious man used all his

powers to win Margaret. He loved her intelligent mind and her sweet beauty, and saw the money she had inherited as only one part of her, although it could help him in his career.

On his way back down from Scotland, he had visited Milton on business connected with Margaret, and it was clear to him that her property there was increasing in value. He was glad that in their new relationship of client and legal adviser, he had many opportunities to talk to her. Margaret was very willing to listen, providing he talked about Milton, and she was delighted that he admired its inhabitants almost more than she did. He praised their energy and their courage, and noticed that when Margaret got bored, if he mentioned Milton her eyes would brighten and she would smile warmly at him.

During her long hours of thinking on the beach, Margaret had realised that her life was her responsibility and no one else's. The result was that when the family returned to London, she told her aunt that she wanted to visit the poor and sick, as she had done in Helstone. Mrs Shaw did not wish to allow this at first, but Margaret was so sweetly persuasive that eventually she agreed. In their private conversations, Edith, Captain Lennox and Mrs Shaw decided that it would be helpful to Henry if Margaret did not go out much socially; Margaret had other admirers but her lack of interest in them was very obvious. They had noticed that Henry was the only man she really enjoyed talking to; and slowly, the two became closer to each other.

## Chapter 14  Meeting Again

Meanwhile, in Milton, Mr Thornton's financial troubles were growing more and more serious. The strike, more than a year and a half ago, had meant that he was unable to complete some of his business contracts. What made things worse was that in recent months, the commercial value of cotton had fallen. Mr Thornton's business was very badly affected and he had spent a lot of money on expensive new machinery, with the result that now he did not have money when he needed it. No new orders were coming in, and meanwhile there were the huge expenses of paying the workers and maintaining the mill.

Mr Thornton did not despair, however. He was as calm and gentle to the women in his home as he had always been. He did not say much to his workers, but they understood his situation and were sympathetic. His relationship with them had changed greatly. Previously, his only ambition had been to be head of a firm that was known and respected all over the world. Now, he often talked to the workers, particularly Higgins, and listened to what they had to say. These conversations had made him realise that people everywhere were connected by the same human feelings. He had begun to see that, as a manufacturer, he was in a position to help and influence those less fortunate than him; he had even arranged to send the older Boucher children to school. Now, though, it seemed that he might lose this position, just as he was beginning to understand it!

One afternoon, as Mr Thornton was walking down Marlborough Street, absorbed in his thoughts, Higgins approached him. Noticing that the mill owner was looking even gloomier than usual, Higgins tried to think of something to cheer him up.

'Have you heard any news of Miss Margaret lately?' he asked.

'Miss – who?' replied Mr Thornton.

'Miss Margaret – Miss Hale, the clergyman's daughter.'

'Oh, Miss Hale!' Suddenly the worried look left Mr Thornton's face and he smiled warmly. 'I'm her tenant now, you know, Higgins. I hear about her from her lawyer every now and then. She's well and living with friends – thank you, Higgins.'

'Will she be coming to Milton again?'

'No.'

Higgins came closer to Mr Thornton and said in a low tone, 'How is the young gentleman?' Seeing that the mill owner did not seem to understand, he continued, 'The young gentleman – I mean Frederick, her brother who came to Milton.'

'He came to Milton!'

'Yes, when their mother died. Don't be afraid I'll tell anyone. Mary told me. She found out about it when she was working at the house.'

'And he was here? It was her brother?'

'Yes. I thought you knew all about it or I would never have said anything. I won't say another word.'

The conversation ended and Mr Thornton continued on his way, saying to himself, 'It was her brother. I am so glad. I may never see her again, but it is a relief to know that. I knew she could never have done anything wrong. But I needed to be sure. I am so glad.'

This news was a little golden thread in his fortunes. Several American firms that he did business with had failed and his financial situation was becoming more and more gloomy. Night after night Mr Thornton took his papers into his office and sat there long after his mother had gone to bed. One morning, when the first light of day was beginning to creep into the room, he realised that nothing could be done; he would have to give up the business that he had worked so hard to make a success.

♦

One hot summer evening, Edith came into Margaret's room, dressed for dinner.

'Margaret, I need to talk to you! Henry has come to me and asked me if a Mr Thornton of Milton – your tenant, you know – can join our dinner party tonight. It is such a nuisance; the arrangements were perfect, and now they must be changed.'

'I won't have dinner tonight. I don't want any,' said Margaret in a low voice. 'Dixon can bring me a cup of tea here. I will be really glad to lie down.'

'You can't do that – we need you! Mr Colthurst, who is a Member of Parliament, is coming, and you know we planned for you to talk to him about Milton. Oh, I've just remembered, this Mr Thornton comes from Milton! How fortunate! Mr Colthurst is going to talk about the cotton industry in his next speech; he and Mr Thornton will have a lot to say to each other. Really, I think Henry has done very well. I asked him if Mr Thornton is a man one should be ashamed of. He said, "Not if you have any sense, little sister." So I suppose he can pronounce his h's.'

'Did Mr Lennox say why Mr Thornton had come to London?' asked Margaret, her voice sounding rather tight.

'Oh, his business has failed, or something like that. I'm sure Henry told you that, the day you had such a headache. Anyway, he has said that Mr Thornton has lost all his money, and deserves our respect, and I must be very polite to him. And as I have no idea how to do that, I need you to help me. And now come down with me, and rest on the sofa for half an hour.'

Henry Lennox came early, and Margaret, blushing as she spoke, asked him some questions about Mr Thornton.

'He can't afford to continue his payments for Marlborough Mills and the house, so he has come to discuss what can be done. I thought you would like him to come to the dinner party.'

Mr Lennox had lowered his voice as he spoke to Margaret. Then, noticing that Mr Thornton had just entered, he jumped up and introduced him to Edith and Captain Lennox. Margaret watched Mr Thornton anxiously as he talked to them. She had not seen him for a long time and his circumstances had changed completely. Being tall and well-built, he looked as impressive as ever, but there were lines of worry on his face that had not been there before. Still, thought Margaret, he had nobleness and strength that made people respect him immediately.

Mr Thornton's first glance around the room had shown him that Margaret was there. He had seen how carefully she listened to Mr Lennox, and came up to her with the calm, friendly manner of an old friend. She blushed, and the colour did not leave her cheeks for the rest of the evening. But she did not seem to have much to say to him, and when others approached her, he moved away and began talking to Mr Lennox.

'Miss Hale is looking very well, is she not?' said Mr Lennox. 'I don't think Milton was very good for her. When she first came to London, I thought I had never seen anyone so changed. Tonight she is looking wonderful, and she is so much stronger now. Last autumn a two–mile walk made her tired. On Friday we walked for six miles at least.'

'We? Who? Just the two of them?' wondered Mr Thornton.

Dinner began, and during the meal Mr Colthurst, the Member of Parliament, heard enough of Mr Thornton's conversation to want to meet him. He asked Edith who the gentleman was, and when she told him that he was Mr Thornton of Milton, exclaimed 'Mr Thornton of Milton!', clearly recognising the name. Edith was pleased. Her dinner party was going well; Henry was being amusing, and Mr Thornton and Mr Colthurst were busy talking in a corner of the room. Margaret did not speak much, but was looking so beautiful that it did not matter. She was watching Mr Thornton's face and noticing the changes in him. He only smiled once, that brilliant smile that she remembered so well, and he glanced at her, almost as if he wanted her approval. But then his expression changed and he avoided looking at her again.

After dinner, the ladies went upstairs, and Margaret, who did not feel like talking, started to do some sewing. The gentlemen soon followed, and as Mr Colthurst and Mr Thornton were standing near her, she was able to listen to their conversation.

'My business has failed,' Mr Thornton said, 'and I am looking for a position in Milton where I can experiment with some ideas that I have.'

'What experiments are these?' asked Mr Colthurst respectfully.

'I now believe that an organisation can be much more successful if the employers and workers talk freely to one another and see each other as people. If an employer has a new plan, the workers may not realise how carefully he has thought about it. But if he discusses it with his workers, they will feel they are part of it and will want it to be successful.'

'And you think this may prevent strikes?'

'Not at all. But it might mean that the strikers aren't so bitter and so full of hatred.'

Suddenly, Mr Thornton turned and walked up to Margaret, as if he knew she was listening.

'Miss Hale,' he said, 'I had a letter from some of my men saying that they wished to work for me if I was ever in a position to employ them again. That was good, wasn't it?'

'Yes, how wonderful! I am so glad,' said Margaret. She looked straight at him with her expressive eyes, then looked down when he looked back at her.

He gazed at her for about a minute, as if he did not know what to say next. Then he sighed and said, 'I knew you would be pleased,' and turned away and did not speak to her again until he wished her good night very formally.

As Mr Lennox was leaving, Margaret said hesitantly, 'Can I speak to you tomorrow? I want your help about – something.'

'Certainly. I will come at whatever time you wish. At eleven? I will see you then.'

His eyes brightened with pleasure. How she was learning to

depend on him! It seemed as if any day now, she would make her feelings about him clear, and then he could once again ask her to marry him.

♦

Edith moved around the house very quietly the next morning, as if any sudden noise would disturb the meeting that was taking place in the sitting-room. Two o'clock came, and Margaret and Mr Lennox still sat there behind closed doors. Then there was the sound of a man's footsteps running downstairs.

Edith opened the sitting-room door.

'Well, Henry?' she said.

'Well what?' he said rather shortly.

'Come in to lunch.'

'No thank you, I can't. I've lost too much time here already.'

'Then it's not all settled,' said Edith sadly.

'No, not at all, if you mean what I think you mean. It will never happen, Edith, so give up thinking about it.'

'If Margaret lived near me, it would be so nice for us all,' said Edith, who did not want Henry to give up hope. 'At the moment, I am always afraid she will go and live in Cadiz.'

'I am certain that Miss Hale would not marry me. And I shall not ask her.'

'Then what have you been talking about?'

'Business matters.'

'Oh, go away if that's all.'

'I shall. I am coming again tomorrow, and bringing Mr Thornton with me, as he needs to talk to Miss Hale.'

'Mr Thornton! Why?'

'He is Miss Hale's tenant,' said Mr Lennox, turning away. 'And he can no longer afford to rent the mill.'

♦

No one ever knew why Mr Lennox did not keep his appointment the following day. Mr Thornton arrived punctually; after he had waited for nearly an hour, Margaret came in looking very white and anxious.

'I am so sorry Mr Lennox is not here,' she said hurriedly. 'He could have done it so much better. He is my adviser in this –'

'I am sorry if it worries you. Shall I try to find him?'

'No, thank you. I wanted to tell you how sorry I am that I am going to lose you as a tenant. But Mr Lennox has told me that he feels sure you will regain your former position. Please don't speak until I have finished.'

Margaret turned over some papers in a trembling, hurried manner, and continued, 'Oh, here it is! He has written a document showing that if you would borrow some money of mine, about £18,000 that is lying unused in the bank, you could pay me better interest than I have now, and Marlborough Mills could continue.'

Mr Thornton did not speak and she went on looking for some papers, as if she was very anxious that he would see the arrangement as being advantageous for her. But her heart almost seemed to stop beating when Mr Thornton said, in a voice that trembled with passion, 'Margaret!'

She looked up and then tried to hide her expressive eyes by hiding her head in her hands. He came nearer, and said her name again in the same passionate way.

Her head sank even lower. He came close to her and knelt by her side, and whispered, 'Be careful. If you do not speak, I shall claim you as my own. Send me away at once, if I must go. Margaret!'

She turned and laid his head on her shoulder, still with her face in her hands. It was delicious for him to feel her soft cheek against him. He held her close, but they did not speak. Finally, she whispered, 'Oh, Mr Thornton, I am not good enough!'

'Not good enough! It is I who am not good enough.'

After a minute or two, he gently removed her hands from her face, and put her arms around his shoulders, as they had been on the day of the riot.

'Do you remember, love?' he asked.

'Yes, and I remember how cruel I was to you the next day.'

'Lift your head. I have something to show you.'

Blushing, she raised her head.

'Do you recognise these roses?' he asked, taking some dead flowers out of a book that he had with him.

'No!' she replied. 'Did I give them to you?'

'No, you did not. But you have probably worn roses like these.'

She looked at them, thought for a minute, then smiled a little and said, 'They are from Helstone, are they not? Oh, have you been there? When did you go?'

'I wanted to see the place where Margaret grew up, even when I had no hope of winning you. I went there after I returned from France.'

'You must give them to me,' she said, trying to take them out of his hand.

'You may have them, but you must pay me for them.'

'How can I ever tell Aunt Shaw?' she whispered, after some minutes of delicious silence.

'Let me speak to her.'

'Oh, no, I should tell her. But what will she say?'

'I can guess. She will exclaim, "That man!".'

'Be careful,' said Margaret, 'or I will imitate the way your mother will say, "That woman!".'

# ACTIVITIES

## Chapters 1–2

*Before you read*

1   Look at the Word List at the back of the book. Check the meaning of the unfamiliar words, then complete the sentences, using a form of a word from the list

    **a**  She … out of the window, watching the scene in the street.

    **b**  'The workers are going to …' said the factory owner, 'and we're going to lose a lot of money.'

    **c**  'Of course, she will … all her uncle's money, since he never married,' said Bella's mother, looking pleased.

    **d**  The … stood at the front of the church, waiting for people to be quiet so that the prayers could begin.

    **e**  Miss Ellis is known to be … . She doesn't speak to people like us.

    **f**  She … when she saw that it was raining and she could not go for her daily walk.

    **g**  He is not a very good … as he often pays the rent late.

    **h**  He did badly in his exams, so he sees a private … after school.

2   Read the Introduction and answer the questions.

    **a**  Who are the two main romantic characters in the novel? Briefly describe their characters and their positions in society when they first appear in the story.

    **b**  Why is the novel called *North and South*?

    **c**  How did Unitarianism influence Gaskell's writing?

    **d**  What do we learn about the conditions of the factory workers and their relations with the cotton mill owners in *North and South*?

*While you read*

3   Are these sentences true (T) or false (F)?

    **a**  Margaret is returning home to her parents after living at her aunt's house for a few years.     .....

101

   **b**  Margaret likes Henry Lennox because many of their
      interests are the same.     .....

   **c**  Edith is getting married very soon.     .....

   **d**  Mrs Hale is discontented because she does not love
      her husband.     .....

   **e**  Margaret refuses Henry Lennox's offer of marriage
      because she only sees him as a friend.     .....

   **f**  Mr Hale has decided to leave the Church of England
      because of financial problems.     .....

   **g**  Mr Hale has decided to move his family to Milton-
      Northern and find work there as a tutor.     .....

   **h**  Mr and Mrs Hale organise the move to Milton-Northern. .....

*After you read*

**4**  Briefly say what you know about:
    Mrs Shaw   Frederick   Dixon   Mr Bell   Helstone

**5**  Explain the relationships between the following characters and
    how these relationships change.
    **a**  Margaret and Edith
    **b**  Margaret and Henry Lennox
    **c**  Mr and Mrs Hale

**6**  Work in pairs. Act out the conversation between Margaret and
    her father towards the end of Chapter 2.

**7**  Answer these questions. Give reasons for your opinions.
    **a**  Has Mr Hale made the right decision to leave the Church
       of England and move his family to Milton-Northern?
    **b**  What is your opinion of Mr Hale? Do you respect him?

**Chapters 3–4**

*Before you read*

**8**  Discuss these questions.
    **a**  How do you think the Hale family's life will change in
       Milton-Northern? What kind of difficulties might they have?
    **b**  What kind of people do you think they might meet there?

**9** Complete the sentences with one or two words.

    **a** Before the family move to Milton-Northern, they stay in a town called ……………... .

    **b** The house they choose in Milton-Northern is in a suburb called …………….. . They do not like the house's ……………... .

    **c** When Margaret meets Mr Thornton, she does not show much ……………... in him.

    **d** When the family move into their new house, Margaret looks for another ……………... but cannot find one.

    **e** Bessy Higgins fears that she will ……………... .

    **f** Margaret does not like Mr Thornton because he is a ……………... .

    **g** Margaret is worried about her mother's ……………... .

    **h** If Frederick returns to England he will probably be ……………... .

*After you read*

  **10** Who is speaking and to whom? What is the speaker talking about?

    **a** 'He is not quite a gentleman – but one would not expect that.'

    **b** 'She'll come, I can see it in her face.'

    **c** 'I hate her!'

    **d** 'And may I say you do not know the north?'

    **e** 'My mother taught me to save a little money each week, and in this way I learnt self-control.'

    **f** 'They say the dust gets into your lungs and you start coughing blood.'

    **g** 'He fought injustice and I am proud of him.'

  **11** Describe:

    **a** Margaret from Mr Thornton's point of view.

    **b** Mr Thornton from Margaret's point of view.

  **12** What are your feelings about these people? Do you like or dislike them? Explain why.

    Margaret    Mr Thornton    Mrs Hale

**Chapters 5–6**

*Before you read*

13 Look at the titles of Chapters 5 and 6 and at the first paragraph of each chapter. What do you think might happen? How do you think the relationship between Margaret and Mr Thornton will develop?

*While you read*

14 Number these events in the correct order, from 1 to 8.

a Dr Donaldson tells Margaret that Mrs Hale is going to die. .....

b Mr Thornton tells the Hales that he sees the workers as children. .....

c Mrs Thornton and Fanny visit the Hales. .....

d Mr Hale tells Mr Thornton about the suffering of the workers. .....

e Mrs Hale nearly dies. .....

f Nicholas Higgins tells Margaret that the workers are striking because the mill owners want to pay them less money. .....

g The Hales send a basket of food to the Boucher family. .....

h Mr Thornton tells his mother that Margaret would never marry him. .....

*After you read*

15 Answer these questions.

a What is Mrs Thornton's reaction to Margaret and why?

b What does Mr Thornton decide he will have to do if the strike continues?

c What do we learn about John Boucher?

d Why doesn't Margaret tell her father the truth about her mother?

e How does Mr Hale learn the truth about his wife's illness?

f Why does Margaret set off for the Thornton's?

**16** Work in pairs. Act out the argument between Margaret and Mr Thornton about the strike and the rights of the workers.

**17** How do you think the part of the story about the Higgins family and the strikers makes the novel more interesting?

## Chapters 7–8

*Before you read*

**18** What do you think will happen to these situations and characters?

    **a** the strike   **b** Mrs Hale   **c** Margaret and Mr Thornton

*While you read*

**19** Circle the correct words.

    **a** The workers break down the *wooden gates / door to Mr Thornton's house.*

    **b** *Mrs Thornton / Margaret* begs Mr Thornton to speak to the workers.

    **c** Mr Thornton has asked the *townspeople / soldiers* for help.

    **d** Margaret is hit by a *shoe / stone.*

    **e** Margaret feels bad because *she is in physical pain / Fanny thinks she is in love with Mr Thornton.*

    **f** Mr Thornton asks Margaret to marry him because he *loves her / wants to save her reputation.*

    **g** Mrs Hale begs Margaret to write to *Frederick / Mrs Shaw.*

    **h** Nicholas is so upset by Bessy's death that Margaret takes him to see *a doctor / Mr Hale.*

    **i** Margaret suggests that Nicholas asks *his old employer / Mr Thornton* for a job.

    **j** When Mr Thornton visits the Hales he *speaks / does not speak* to Margaret.

*After you read*

**20** Describe the response of the following people to the riot and say what it reveals about their characters.

    Margaret    Mr Thornton    Fanny    Mrs Thornton

**21** Describe Margaret's response to Mr Thornton's offer of marriage and Mr Thornton's reaction and behaviour afterwards.

**22** Discuss these questions. Give reasons for your opinions.

    **a** Who do you feel most sympathetic towards, Margaret or Mr Thornton?

    **b** Do you think Margaret was right to write to Frederick? What would you have done in her position?

    **c** Which part of these chapters interests you most?

## Chapters 9–10

*Before you read*

**23** Answer these questions.

    **a** If Frederick returns, what do you think might happen?

    **b** How do you think Margaret and Mr Thornton's relationship will progress?

*While you read*

**24** Who is it? Write the name of the character who …

    **a** promises to be a friend to Margaret? ...............

    **b** surprises Margaret by arriving one evening? ...............

    **c** warns Margaret about Leonards? ...............

    **d** pushes Leonards so that he falls? ...............

    **e** quietly attends Mrs Hale's funeral? ...............

    **f** tells Margaret that she may have to appear at an inquest? ...............

    **g** saves Margaret from appearing in court? ...............

    **h** fears being despised for lying? ...............

    **i** sends a book but does not come to visit? ...............

*After you read*

**25** What happens in these chapters between:

    **a** Frederick and Mrs Hale?

    **b** Dixon and Leonards?

    **c** Frederick and Leonards?

    **d** Inspector Watson and Margaret?

**26** Describe how:

    **a** Mr Thornton shows his great love for Margaret.

    **b** Margaret's feelings about Mr Thornton change.

**27** In what ways does Frederick's part in the story make it more interesting? Give reasons for your opinion.

## Chapters 11–12

*Before you read*

**28** Look at the titles of these chapters. What do you think might happen in them?

*While you read*

**29** Number these in the correct order, from 1 to 7.

a Margaret learns that Mrs Boucher is dying. .....

b Mr Hale dies. .....

c Mrs Thornton visits Margaret. .....

d Mr Bell writes a letter to Margaret. .....

e Mr Thornton asks Margaret for an explanation for her lie. .....

f Mr Bell tells Mr Thornton about Frederick. .....

g Mr Bell makes his first visit to the Hales'. .....

*After you read*

**30** Answer these questions.

a What most upsets Mr Thornton about Margaret's lie?

b Why does Mr Thornton offer Higgins a job?

c When Mr Thornton comes to tea with the Hales and Mr Bell, what does he say that upsets Margaret so much?

d What does Frederick say in his letters to Margaret?

e How does Mr Bell say that he will look after Margaret?

f What happens as a result of Mr Hale's death?

**31** Work in pairs. Act out the following conversation.

*Student A*: You are Margaret. Talk about your relationship with Mr Thornton, how your feelings towards him have changed and if there is any hope for the relationship.

*Student B*: You are a friend of Margaret. Listen, ask questions, and express your opinions.

**32** What is your opinion of Mr Thornton's behaviour towards Margaret in these chapters? Give reasons for your answer.

**Chapters 13–14**

*Before you read*

**33** Answer these questions.

   **a** What do you think will happen when Margaret meets Henry Lennox again?

   **b** Do you think Margaret and Mr Thornton will meet again? If so, how?

*While you read*

**34** Complete the sentences with one or two words.

   **a** Although life in Harley Street is luxurious, Margaret feels ................. .

   **b** When Mr Bell dies, Margaret becomes a ................. woman.

   **c** Margaret and ................. start becoming closer to each other.

   **d** Mr Thornton learns the truth about ................. from Higgins.

   **e** Mr Thornton has to give up his ................. .

   **f** At Edith's dinner party, Mr Thornton has a conversation about his new ideas with ................. .

   **g** Margaret offers to lend Mr Thornton ................. .

   **h** Mr Thornton shows Margaret some ................. from Helstone.

*After you read*

**35** What role does Henry Lennox play in these chapters?

**36** List the changes that mean that Margaret and Mr Thornton are able to come together at last.

**37** Answer these questions. Give reasons for your answers.

   **a** Do you find the ending satisfying?

   **b** Do you think Margaret and Mr Thornton will be happy together?

   **c** How do you feel about Henry Lennox? Do you feel sorry for him? Why (Why not)?

## Writing

**38** Discuss the following statement:

'Margaret and Mr Thornton needed to learn from each other before they could come together.'

**39** Describe the parts that three of these characters play in the story:

Frederick    Dixon    Mr Bell    Edith    Mrs Thornton

**40** Write a newspaper report describing the riot in Marlborough Street.

**41** Explain the part that Nicholas and Bessy Higgins play in the novel. What was the aim of Elizabeth Gaskell in introducing them, in your opinion?

**42** Write a description of Margaret, describing how she changes. Say how you feel about her. Give reasons for your opinion.

**43** Tell the story from the point of view of Henry Lennox.

**44** Discuss the following statement:

'North and South is much more than a romantic novel. It is a serious study of important social issues of the time.'

**45** Say whether you agree with the following statement, giving reasons for your opinion:

'Mr Hale is a weak man.'

**46** Describe Mr Thornton from the point of view of Nicholas Higgins.

**47** Write a letter from Margaret to Edith describing her life in Milton-Northern after she has married Mr Thornton.

# WORD LIST

**be absorbed** (v) to be very interested in something that you are doing
**alibi** (n) proof that a person was somewhere else at the time of a crime
**blush** (v) to become red in the face with embarrassment
**clergyman** (n) a priest in a Christian church
**contempt** (n) a strong feeling that another person is worthless
**despair** (v) to feel that you have no hope at all
**despise** (v) to hate someone and have no respect for them
**disdain** (n) a lack of respect for someone
**distressed** (adj) extremely upset and unhappy
**exclaim** (v) to say something suddenly and loudly
**gaze** (n/v) a long look at someone or something
**gloom** (n) a feeling of sadness and lack of hope
**haughty** (adj) proud and unfriendly
**inherit** (v) to receive property or money from someone after they die
**inquest** (n) an official enquiry into why someone has died
**interest** (n) money charged or paid for a loan
**mutiny** (n/v) a refusal by a group of people to accept someone in authority
**passion** (n) a very strong feeling of love or desire
**porter** (n) someone whose job is to carry bags
**riot** (n) an event in a public place when a crowd of people behave violently
**scornfully** (adv) with a feeling of great disrespect
**shawl** (n) a large piece of cloth worn around a woman's shoulders
**sigh** (n/v) a loud breath out from your mouth that expresses your unhappiness, tiredness or disappointment
**sob** (v) to cry noisily while taking short breaths
**stately** (adj) formal and impressive
**strike** (n/v) a refusal to work by people who want better pay or working conditions
**sympathy** (n) a feeling that you understand someone's problems
**tenant** (n) someone who rents a house or other property from the owner
**tutor** (n) someone who gives private lessons in a subject
**vicarage** (n) the house of a priest in the Church of England